THE FUTURE OF THE CORPORATION

THE FUTURE OF THE CORPORATION

Edited by

HERMAN KAHN

 Mason & Lipscomb PUBLISHERS   NEW YORK

To the late Knut Laurin, president of PLM 1943–1970, one of the great men in packaging and a pioneer in long-range planning, whose dedication and foresight created the X80 seminar,

and

to Ulf Laurin, appointed president of PLM in 1970, who so faithfully and successfully realized his father's idea

Contents

Introduction

Over the past generation, corporate executives and other businessmen have become increasingly aware of the need for better information, techniques, and mechanisms for dealing with rapid economic, cultural, social, and political change. Both modern industrial societies and the less developed nations will undergo novel strains and challenges that seem certain to influence the next decade in quite significant ways, and the 1980s in perhaps fundamental respects. Multinational, international, and national corporations are all likely to find it increasingly desirable, even indispensable, to prepare for what will happen during and after the present decade. While the requirement to prepare adequately for environmental changes critical to the operations of almost any given corporation is increasingly being recognized, the question of *how* to go about this, of how to appraise realistically the impact of major trends and developments and the possible advantages or disadvantages of various actions that might be taken today, nevertheless remains one of the most perplexing problems of corporate leadership today.

Traditionally most corporations have devoted relatively little attention to the long-range future. Often enough, corporate planning has not gone beyond goal-setting, budgeting, and requirements for current and near-term operations. When attention has been directed

1

more than five years ahead, the result has seldom been better than a straightforward extrapolation of current trends and activities. Even where this has been done well, the results have rarely been sufficient for direct use in decision making.

For these and many other reasons, corporations have tended in the past to place severe limits on the time period and range of use of their future planning; the number and complexity of factors and the many uncertainties affecting the corporation's future simply made it too difficult to form sound—or even useful—judgments about conditions more than five years ahead. For most corporate decisions it has been wiser to wait—to defer anticipatory reactions until conditions evolved further, even if this did risk missing a bus or two. Thus many future possibilities were understood to be important, but were also considered—often correctly—to be too general or uncertain or confusing to warrant serious, independent, informed study by any one company, even a large one. Only an occasional joint enterprise—or an essentially academic research project supported by large grants—ordinarily could muster the necessary intellectual and financial resources.

Because of the current and projected rapidity of change and because this change may be of a fundamental nature, it is evident that many corporations are today, and most will be tomorrow, increasingly interested in searching for more effective means for anticipating medium and long-range issues and trends. For many corporations the problems that a changing world will bring in the next decade or two may be particularly acute. Even the most effective long-range planning, of course, will not enable a corporation to make practical decisions today that would avoid problems entirely or anticipate changes precisely: at the very minimum, however, longer-range and more systematic planning and thinking should make some anticipatory reactions possible with continuing, realistic planning and modification of plans, to hedge against both good and bad eventualities and to improve the organization's ability to react rapidly and appropriately to many, if not most, of the prospective changes and new issues.

To pay sustained and systematic attention to the potentialities—the hazards and opportunities—of the seventies and eighties as they arise, may or may not result in decisions that affect current and day-to-day operations; but this thinking should at least produce insights into the areas in which corporate leadership should begin to consider the possibilities of major change and to chart alternatives. An additional, often overlooked, yet almost equally important result of thinking about the 1975–85 time-period, is that it can also stimulate and stretch the imagination of the individuals or management groups involved, increasing the ability of top management to identify and understand the significance of new patterns and crises, and improving management's speed, flexibility, and effectiveness in both the making and carrying out of decisions.

This book stems from a conference specifically designed to address some of the most perplexing and least understood of the new issues that are likely to affect the corporation and its environment in the seventies and eighties. The conference at Malmo, Sweden, in June 1970 was sponsored by the PLM (Aktiebolaget Platmanufaktur) Corporation to mark its fiftieth anniversary. The intention of the endeavor is perhaps well summed up by these remarks made by Mr. Sven-Eric Nilsson, a member of the Swedish Cabinet, toward the close of the proceedings:

"Those who live to an old age are often prone to look back at their youth and successful maturity. This disposition is particularly evident at a jubilee, if memory has not become to much dimmed by age and if the vigor of manhood has not been substituted by infirmity. The jubilee celebrator will ask himself first of all *why* he has become so old and successful while others have missed the boat. The correct answer to this question will often be—foresight. If the jubilee celebrator wishes to go on living and have continual success, he will conclude that he should immediately leave memories behind and look forward. His interest should be concentrated on the future. Therefore it is proof of the vitality of the company which is our host that it has chosen to celebrate its fiftieth anniversary by arranging this seminar devoted to the future.

"It is really an impressive team of prophets that the company has managed to assemble on this occasion. The names alone testify that here will have been presented the leading edge of the art of 'futures research.' The implication of this term has not yet been fully stabilized. More or less long-term prognoses have, of course, been made in different fields for a long time. What is happening now is no doubt that the quantitative and qualitative possibilities of making long-term prognoses are increasing at a rapid rate, that the working methods are developing, and that the necessity of an integration between the different fields of prognosis are making themselves felt.

"In this connection, researchers' concerns with the future have already achieved a good deal, but a tremendous lot still remains as regards possibilities and tasks. For the (Swedish) society which I represent here, it is important that the results of futures research will be to the benefit of the society as a whole and all its parts. What is important is to differentiate between research and the decision functions of the society. Prognosis tends to have a guiding effect. If that is the case, the researchers will have taken over the tasks which belong to the citizens and the social decision process. But if the citizens do not have access to the material under development in the future and the consequences of different action alternatives which the researcher workers can provide, then the citizens will be acting in the dark. Thus it is of important social interest that research about the future is developed so as to promote the freedom of citizens to choose the political goals and their potentials to reach their goals. These views indicate a need of the society to take an interest in the questions about the aims for research on the future and how it should be organized. Also, the connection between research for long-term planning for the society and the democratic decision process needs scrutinizing. These questions are at present being examined by my government. When I speak here about the interest of society in the development of research regarding the future, I have not only the public sector in mind. The future of each branch of industry and each individual firm is dependent on the whole future social environment where the industry shall develop and the firm shall work. Prognoses only for isolated sectors or firms are therefore of limited value. The social integration of research regarding the future is thus also in the interest of the industry and trade.

"Our research regarding the future must also be international. This is due to the fact that our Swedish society is only a part of the world community and that our development cannot be separated from the international development. But it is also due to the fact that we must avail ourselves of the research-results and the research methods which are developed in other countries. For this reason I think it is particularly valuable that so many of the most prominent in the world within this field have been willing to come to our country to impart to us their knowledge and their views. But of course we should also be grateful to our host-company that has taken so much interest in our future as to arrange this seminar on this very high level."

The conference generated a sense of intellectual excitement, creativity, and an appealing combination of fun and serious work. Part of this was because of the magnificent care, efforts, and hospitality of Ulf Laurin, president of PLM, and of Jan Sahlberg, the executive director and coordinator of the conference; part because of the intelligent, gracious, firm, and *just* chairing of Tore Browaldh; and part because of the nature of the subject and the surprisingly intense and informed interest taken by both the contributors and the audience in the issues presented and in the subsequent discussion. It was a great pleasure for me to accept the invitation of the

P.L.M. management to help in organizing the conference and to edit the proceedings (and here I very much appreciate the assistance of B. Bruce-Briggs of the Hudson Institute).

It is now more or less commonplace that the advanced economies of the world are entering something that is often described as the "post-industrial culture." The first three contributors at the conference focused their remarks on this change in our culture, emphasizing, however, different perspectives and aspects of the change.

Thus, Daniel Bell (who actually coined the term "post-industrial")* started by defining and then discussing the basic nature of this new development in man's history. He then went on to emphasize the importance and character of the "knowledge industry," the new technical elites, some of the new technologies and the growing importance of "science-based" industries, and, finally, new methods and issues in education. I also discussed some of the technological issues and changing value systems, but with a focus on what I feel are some of the most important international and domestic developments that reflect the many changes or modifications that are becoming evident today. Peter Drucker gave a magnificent presentation on the central role management and the multinational corporations are likely to play in the future—in particular, the dramatic impact that proper leadership and entrepreneurship may have in resolving or otherwise dealing with many of the issues

*See his article in *The Public Interest* (Winter 1967) and Bell, *The Coming of Post-Industrial Society* (New York: Basic Books, 1973).

and problems of today—issues that seem largely insoluble and intractable by current and customary institutional arrangements and programs. He points out that in some ways management is the success story of the twentieth century, having successfully created a new function, a new discipline, and a new leadership group, and by these means played a central role in many, if not all, of the current achievements of industrial society. With luck and skill, he argues, management should do as well in the future in resolving most of the remaining problems.

As discussed later, the four other contributors—Ota Sik, Donald C. Burnham, Torgny Segerstedt, and Hisamichi Kano—addressed special issues related to the overall theme. It is, of course, impossible in one conference to study "everything" in depth. Therefore, we relegated many general issues to two special discussion sessions. On the whole, both in the discussion and in the assignment of talks, there was an attempt to be comprehensive rather than specialized, and to focus attention on the most basic changes likely to make important differences to the business environment. Thus, with the exceptions noted below, the emphasis was on broad relevance and contextual analysis rather than details; on possible developments likely to change the basic conditions and assumptions that underlie corporate operations and decision making today, such as the role of profit and salary as a primary individual motivation, executive loyalty to the firm placed above most other interests, the economic-political primacy of industrial culture, etc., which are so basic to present-day thinking that they are often automatically accepted as constants. Little explicit or even conscious acknowledgment is made of the fact that they have evolved from the past environment and, like that past environment, are themselves subject to modification and replacement.

Political institutions and political problems also change. Ota Sik took an activist position on one of the most important of these problems—and one that had long threatened to become a more or less permanent institution—the great schism in Europe that we normally denote by the term "Iron Curtain." Sik suggested that since there was a trend among the socialist economies toward use of market mechanisms and market pricing, and an even stronger trend toward planning in the capitalist countries, there might well result a conversion between the two systems, at least for many important economic and political purposes. Sik's thesis aroused a great deal of discussion among European newspapers—being at least as widely reported as the other talks at the conference. Whether or not one wholly agrees with Professor Sik, tribute must be paid to the importance of his endeavors—and his analyses—in trying to build a bridge over the great schism in Europe. In fact, many would interpret recent events involving East-West relations as confirming his main concept. Although he begins with a Marxist framework probably quite strange to most readers of this book, he ends with urging systematic profit-sharing along lines quite similar to those advocated by capitalist defenders. Moreover, his theoretical discussion of attempts to resolve the "contradictions" between the interests of individual firms and the entire society by means of overall planning together with producer participation is remarkably relevant to the problems of huge corporations in trying to promote corporate goals and at the same time maintain the initiative and incentives of divisional and plant management.

Another emphasis of the conference concerned those aspects of change that normal forecasting techniques and planning staffs have difficulty handling. For example, a fundamental point, often neglected in economic projections and technological forecasts, is that people are changing, both in terms of individual character and personality and of political and social cultures. These changes are rooted in the growing secularization of most societies, various consequences of new technology and new politics, the growth of affluence, and the spread of education. Since these trends interact with each other and may gain momentum, they may have cumulative effects: quantitative changes can result in substantial qualitative differences. In particular, Torgny Segerstedt in his 1985 Swedish scenarios managed to bring to life many of the above possibilities, though some of the other participants expressed disagreement on some of his detailed predictions.

At this two-day conference we could not discuss all of the issues we wished to raise, but we managed at least to touch on a surprising number of them in the talks already mentioned. In addition, D. C. Burnham in particular focused attention on what he called the "four keys to 1980" and summarized four major precepts that management must follow if it is to operate well in the world just described. Thus he emphasized the necessity for increased productivity "to pay" for the many new needs and the enlarged tertiary and quaternary services; the rigorous requirements for "excellence" in all aspects of execution and operation to meet the new and exacting criteria; and, finally and most important, to become both "consumer-oriented" and "involved in the community" sufficiently intensely so as to be able to deal empathetically and effectively with the changing values and attitudes. Finally, the formal presentations were ended by Hisamichi Kano, who discussed the most economically successful country of all, Japan, and the special cultural and business traits that have enabled this prodigy of development to perform so spectacularly well in the postwar period.

HERMAN KAHN

DANIEL BELL, born in 1919, graduated from the City College of New York in 1938 with a bachelor's degree in social sciences and received his Ph.D. at Columbia University in 1960. In the early 1940s he was Managing Editor of *The New Leader;* Instructor in Social Science at the University of Chicago, 1945–48; Labor Editor of *Fortune Magazine,* 1948–58; Professor of Sociology at Columbia University, 1959–68.

Dr. Bell is Chairman of the Commission on the Year 2000 of the American Academy of Arts and Sciences. He is on the editorial boards of *Daedalus* and *Labor History,* and Co-Editor of *The Public Interest.*

Among his books are *History of Marxian Socialism in the United States* (1952), *Work and Its Discontents* (1956), *The End of Ideology* (1960), *The Reforming of General Education* (1966), *Towards the Year 2000* (editor) (1968), *Confrontation* (1969), *Capitalism Today* (1971), and *The Coming of Post-Industrial Society* (1973).

The Post-Industrial Society—
Expectations for the
1970s and 1980s
DANIEL BELL

It was once exceedingly rare to observe the formation of institutions *de novo*. Social change was crescive and slow moving. Adaptations were piecemeal and contradictory, the process of diffusion halting, the spread of rationalization difficult and cumbersome. In his reflections on history, forty years ago, Paul Valéry, the quintessential Frenchman of letters, pointed out the absence from history books of major phenomena which were imperceptible owing to the slowness of their evolution.[1] "An event which takes shape over a century will not be found in any document or collection of memoirs," he remarked. Valéry had in mind the discovery of electricity and the conquest of the world by its applications. "Electricity in Napoleon's day had about the same importance as, in the days of Tiberius, could have been ascribed to Christianity." Yet the gradual electrification of the world was more fraught with consequences, and has been more responsible for the modification of life, than the political events which are the foci of the historian's concern.

What is true of a technological innovation is true of a social process as well. Where, and at what time, did any contemporary writer notice the decline of feudalism and

13

the rise of a capitalist economy? A process so long and complicated has no single "birth year" to mark its emergence. There are seldom single "turning points," such as a political revolution, to signal the transformation of a society.

A consciousness of change took hold in the nineteenth century. History, declared a number of social thinkers, is a determinate process, and various individuals sought to chart the movement of society by identifying qualitatively different periods of historical time. Comte, organizing his scheme around the progress of beliefs, sketched a movement from religious through metaphysical to positive (or scientific) thought. Marx, using a combination of property relations and productive power, described the changes from slavery to feudalism to capitalism and prophesied socialism as the next historical phase for civilization. Sir Henry Maine, looking at legal relations, described the evolution of modern society as moving from status to contract.

In our day, we have lost the belief in a single-minded notion of a linear social evolution and the idea of some fixed determinateness. History is more variable and recalcitrant in its response to the *demiourgos* of spirit or technology. There is, in addition—and it may be our *hubris*, to be chided as such by future generations—a belief that men can intervene and direct a social process. Perhaps the most important social change of our time is the effort toward the deliberate contrivance of social change. Men now seek to anticipate change, measure the course of its direction and its impact, control it, and even shape it for predetermined ends. "The transformation of society" is no longer an abstract phrase but a process in which governments are actively engaged on a highly conscious basis. The industrialization of Japan by the old Samurai class was an action aimed at transforming an agrarian economy from the top, and it succeeded remarkably because of the disciplined nature of the social relationships that existed in post-Meji restoration society. The extraordinary upheavals in the Soviet Union, more ruthless and more concentrated in time than the changes in any other society in history, were carried out on the basis of specific plans in which the movements of population, as well as industrial targets, were plotted on social charts. The breakup of the old colonial system since the end of World War II has brought about the creation of more than seventy new countries, many of them committed abstractly to the idea of socialism, in which the creation of new industrial and urban economies is the self-conscious aim of new elites. And in the older western societies we have seen the emergence of the idea of planning in more differentiated form, whether it be target plans, indicative planning, induced investment or directed economic growth, as part of the effort to control change. In all this, a new mentality has been created, that of the technocrat, with an emphasis on functional rationality, economizing and maximization, planning and foresight. And this, too, is part of the distinctiveness of the time.

The Post-Industrial Society

Within this historical context I propose to you that what is emerging is what I have called a "post-industrial society." Let me be abstract for a moment and then try to be more specific. If one speculates on the shape of society forty of fifty years from now or what emerges in the present, it becomes clear that the "old" industrial order is passing and a "new" society is in the making. To speak rashly: if the dominant figures of the past hundred years have been the entrepreneur, the businessman, and the industrial executive, the new men are the scientists, the mathematicians, the economists, and the engineers of the new computer technology and those organizations which transform themselves into research-minded organizations. The dominant institutions of the new society—in the sense that they will provide the most creative challenges and enlist the richest talents—will be the intellectual institutions. The leadership of the new society will rest not with the businessmen and the corporation as we know them (for a good deal of production will have been routinized), but with research corporations, industrial laboratories, experimental stations and the universities—and the political executives and administrators who will manage these.

To say that the primary institutions of the new age will be intellectual is not to say that the majority of persons will be scientists, engineers, technicians, or intellectuals. The majority of individuals in contemporary society are not businessmen, yet one can say that this has been a "business civilization." The basic values of society have been focused on business institutions, the largest rewards have been in business, and the strongest power has been held by the business community, although today that power is shared within the economic order, by the trade union and regulated, in some extent, by the political order. In the most general ways, however, the major decision affecting the day-to-day life of the citizens—the kinds of work available, the location of plants, investment decisions on new production, the distribution of tax burdens, occupational mobility—have been made by business, and, in many countries, more recently, by government, though with a major priority, still, to the welfare of business.

To say that the major institutions of the new society will be intellectual is to say that production and business decisions will be subordinated to, or will derive from other forces in society; that the crucial decisions regarding the growth of the economy and its balance will come from government, but these will be based on government's sponsorship of research and development, of cost-effectiveness and cost-benefit analysis; that the making of decisions, because of the intricately linked nature of their consequences, will have an increasingly technical character. The husbanding of talent and the spread of educational and intellectual institutions will become a prime concern for the society; not only the best talents, but eventually the entire complex of prestige and status will be rooted in the intellectual and scientific communities.

In sketching a broad picture of the post-industrial society, let me quickly stipulate the limits. The idea of a post-industrial society is not intended to be, nor is it, a "complete" picture of a complex society. Societies vary by culture, values, national character, historical traditions and political interests and capabilities. Today, e.g., the United States, the Soviet Union, Germany—in its Nazi phase and now as a divided society, capitalist west and communist east—and Japan are all industrial societies, but they are organized politically and sociologically in different ways. Nor would I claim that the new men of the post-industrial society would become the rulers of such a society; I do not believe that technocrats or scientists ever could achieve that power. In every modern society, the political system is paramount and the managers of the political system, representing different constituencies, rule.

The post-industrial concept is an effort to identify *crucial structural trends* in the society—trends in the economic, technological, and occupational pictures and in the *sources of innovation* in society. But these can be managed in various ways. In short, one can predict a broad historical trend, but not the exact configurations of its organization.

The Dimensions of a Post-Industrial Society

I have said that the post-industrial concept is an effort to identify basic trends in the social structures of advanced industrial countries. One can specify five such dimensions or attributes which, together, compose this idea of a post-industrial society. These are:

- (a) The change from a goods producing to a service economy.
- (b) The preeminence of the professional and technical class in the society.
- (c) The centrality of *theoretical knowledge* as the source of innovation and policy formulation in the society.
- (d) The creation of a new "intellectual technology."
- (e) The possibility of a self-sustaining technological growth.

Let's look at these in order.

(a) The service economy

More than twenty-five years ago, Colin Clark, in his *Conditions of Economic Progress,* classified economies on the basis of sectors which he defined as primary, secondary, and tertiary. The primary were those essentially in the extractive fields; the secondary, manufacturing or industrial; the tertiary, services. By that criterion, the first and simplest dimension of a post-industrial society is that the majority of the labor force no longer be engaged in primary or secondary sectors, but in services, which are defined, residually, as trade, finance, transport, recreation, health, education, research, and government.

One can divide the world into three different kinds of sectors. The first might be called those in extractive industries. The overwhelming number of the countries in the world today are still in the primary sector, agriculture, mining, fishing, and forestry. These are economies based directly on natural resources. Their productivity is low and the prices of their products subject to wide fluctuation of world markets. Most of the world is still in this agrarian phase. In Africa and in Asia, more than 70 per cent of the population live in such agrarian societies. Most of Latin America is primarily agrarian, with the high percentage of services engaged either in households or small mercantile trade.

In a small portion of the world—in western and northern Europe, the Soviet Union, and Japan—a major portion of the labor force is engaged in manufacturing. Here productivity rises at a fairly constant rate and national incomes tend to rise fairly steadily. These are industrialized societies.

By this token, namely the distribution of the labor force, the United States is the first post-industrial society in that the service sector accounts for more than half of the total employment and more than half the gross national product. It is the first nation in which the major portion of the population is engaged neither in agrarian nor in industrial pursuits. Shortly after the turn of this century, only 3 in every 10 workers were in service industries. By 1950, the weight had shifted to just over 5 in every 10. By 1968, the proportion was almost 6 in every 10. And by 1980, according to the projections of the U.S. Department of Labor, of a 100 million person labor force in U.S., almost 7 out of every 10 workers (about 68 million) will be in service industries.[2] This is a major shift from a goods-producing society to a service economy. And this is a picture which foreshadows the path of every industrial society.

Are these tendencies "inevitable"? There is no inevitable force for nations to industrialize; this depends upon their ability to create entreprenurial and managerial classes and to institutionalize mechanisms which create savings in the economy and translate these savings into investment. But once nations do industrialize, there is a "trajectory" which leads them, as in the case of the United States, to a general shift from goods production to services. This derives from two factors. One is the sectoral differences in productivity, where the steady introduction of labor-saving devices leads to a *relative* reduction of employment in manufacturing. Second, as national income rises, there is, invariably, a greater demand for education, health, recreation, and the like, and the greater proportion of the labor force moves into the service sector. Thus one can say that this is a general structural tendency in all advanced industrial countries.

(b) The Professional and Technical Class

The second way of defining a post-industrial society is by the change in occupational pattern, i.e., not only the industry *where* people work, but the *kind* of work they do.

The onset of industrialization brought with it a new phenomenon, the semiskilled worker, the man who can be trained easily within a few weeks, to do the simple routine operations required in machine work. Within industrial societies, the semiskilled worker has been the single largest occupational category in the labor force. The expansion of the tertiary economy, however, with its emphasis on trade, finance, education, and government has inevitably brought about a shift to white-collar occupations. In the United States in 1956 the number of white-collar workers for the first time in the history of industrial civilization outnumbered the number of blue-collar workers. Since then the ratio has been widening steadily; today, white-collar workers outnumber the blue-collar by more than five to four; by 1980 it will be five to three.

But the most startling—and important—change has been the growth of professional and technical employment, in occupations which usually require some college education. In the United States in 1890 there were less than a million of these persons. In 1940 there were 3.9 million; in 1964 the number had risen to 8.6 million, and by 1980 there will be 15.5 million, making it the second single largest of the occupational divisions of the country, exceeded, in absolute numbers, only by the semiskilled workers; but that latter category is shrinking, relative to the others.

And within that component the major change has been the extraordinary rise of scientists and engineers who form the key in the post-industrial society. For while the growth rate of the professional and technical class has been *double* that of the labor force as a whole, the growth rate of scientists and engineers has been *triple* that of the working population as a whole. By 1975, for example, the United States will have about two million engineers, compared with approximately 850,000 in 1960.

Again, these changing patterns in the distribution of the labor force are intrinsic to the changes of industrial economies, and we can expect the same pattern to manifest itself, in varying degree, in the advanced industrial societies.

(c) The Primacy of Theoretical Knowledge

In identifying a new and emerging social structure, it is not only in the extrapolated social trends such as the question of section distribution or occupation distribution—or the creation of a service economy, or the expansion of the professional and technical classes—that one seeks to understand fundamental social change. It is in some specifically defining characteristic—the ganglion, so to speak, of a social system—which becomes the organizing principle around which institutions change and develop. A capitalist society has as a basic organizing principle that of property and usually private property.

The defining characteristic of industrial society has been the organization of machines for the production of goods; and in this respect capitalism and socialism are two variants of industrial society. The post-industrial society, however, is organized around *knowledge*, and this gives rise to new social relationships and new structures which have to be organized politically.

Now, knowledge has been necessary for the existence of any society. But what is distinctive and new about the post-industrial society is the change in the character of knowledge itself. For what has now become decisive for the organization of decisions and the control of change is the centrality of *theoretical* knowledge—the primacy of theory over empiricism, and the codification of knowledge into abstract systems of symbols that can guide practice in many and different and varied circumstances.

One can see this principally in the new relation of science to technology, in the new intimately linked character of the two, a point which I shall expand in a short while. In a less direct but equally important way, this changing relation between theory and empiricism is reflected in the management of economies. In this respect, it is striking to compare the self-confidence of governments forty years ago and today in regard to economic policy. In reading the memoirs of politicians and economists, one realizes that forty years ago, during the height of the Great Depression, few of them had any notions how to bring their economies out of such a crisis. It was largely the theorists who gave guidance. (Interestingly, it was Sweden which pointed the way, in the policy of

Ernest Wigforss, at that time the minister of finance, helped by the so-called "Swedish school" of economists, principally Gunnar Myrdal and Erik Lindhal.) The rise of macroeconomists and the new codifications of economic theory now allow governments to intervene in economic matters in order to shape economic growth, redirect the allocation of resources, maintain balances between different sectors, and even, as in the case of Great Britain, where the Labour government deliberately engineered a controlled recession in order to redeploy resources, all based, rightly or wrongly, on some conceptions of theory.

But the central point remains—in the nature of innovation, and the formulation of policy—advances in the economy, and in science and technology today, depend *primarily* on the codification of theoretical knowledge and, therefore, on the institutions—universities, academies, and research institutes and laboratories—where such codification takes place.

(d) The New "Intellectual Technology"

Fourth in this catalogue of the characteristics of the new post-industrial society is the emergence of a new "intellectual technology," which by the end of the twentieth century may be as decisive in human affairs as the machine technology has been in the past century and a half.

By an "intellectual technology," I mean such varied techniques as linear programming, systems analysis, information theory, decision theory, game theory, and simulation, all of this linked to the computer, which extend our intellectual powers enormously. We can through various programming devices create various scheduling and queuing matrices which create more orderly production programs, or which manage "batch" and "mix" tasks in production. We can, with these techniques, accumulate and manipulate large aggregates of data, of a differentiated kind, so as to have a more complete knowledge of social and economic matters. On a more sophisticated level, we can, through simulation, create "controlled experiments" in the social sciences in order to trace out the progressive and regressive consequences of alternative choices of action—such as in city planning—and create models, such as econometric and forecasting models of the economy which can rapidly "solve" the thousands of simultaneous equations necessary for an understanding of changes in the economy.

In short, we have here the basic tools for the necessary planning and the organization of a society and for help in the formulation of social policy.

(e) Self-Sustaining Technological Growth

And finally, through new techniques in technological forecasting, we may be able to achieve a new dimension of societal change, the creation of a self-sustaining technological growth. Modern industrial society became possible when economies were able to create new institutional mechanisms to build up savings (through banks, insurance companies, equity capital through the stock market, and government debt) and to use these pools of money for investment purposes. The ability to reinvest regularly at least ten per cent of the gross national product became the basis of what W. W. Rostow called the "take-off" point for economic growth.

A modern society, however, in order to avoid stagnation or "maturity" (however that vague word is defined) has to open up new technological frontiers in order to maintain productivity and expansion. The development of new forecasting and "mapping techniques"—a further point to be discussed below—may make possible a new phase in economic history, the conscious, planned advance of technological growth.

If one sums up, at this point, an image of a post-industrial society, one can do so, schematically by looking at my triad of concepts:

—A preindustrial society lives, primarily, as a "game against nature," it is dependent on natural resources and raw labor force, and growth is limited by population and land.

—An industrial society is, largely, a "game against fabricated nature," dependent primarily on energy sources, and growth is largely dependent on the function of the creation of mass production and mass markets.

—A post-industrial society is a "game between persons," dependent largely on "information" (using the word in its technical-communication-theory sense), and its growth is a function of the codification of theoretical knowledge.

The Role of Science-Based Industries

As should be now clear, central for me in this conception of the post-industrial society is this idea of codification of theoretical knowledge, and this is most evident in the changed relation of science to technology, with consequences crucial to all advanced industrial economies.

If one looks at the industries which are still central in society today—steel, electricity, telephone, telegraph, automobile, aviation—curiously enough these are all *nineteenth*-century industries (though steel was "discovered" in the eighteenth century and aviation in the twentieth, but nineteenth-century industries in their pattern of their unfolding and development). That is, they were all shaped by inspired and talented tinkerers—Darby in steel, Siemens and Edison in electricity, Bell in telephony, Morse in telegraphy, Marconi in wireless, the Wright brothers in aviation—all of whom worked quite independently of the fundamental work going on in science at the time. Edison, a genius in his way, was quite indifferent to the work of Maxwell and Faraday in electromagnetism and cared not one whit for theory.

The first *modern*, or genuinely twentieth-century, industry is chemistry, in that its inventions, the chemically created synthetics, necessarily are based on the theoretical properties of the macromolecules one has to manipulate in order to achieve the planned creation of new products. In effect, what is obvious and characteristic about the nature of modern industry is its dependence on research and on science. As Nelson, Peck, and Kalachek have observed, if one compares Watt's utilization of the theory of latent heat in his invention of the separate condensing chamber for steam engines, or Marconi's exploitation of the developments in electromagnetism with the work, e.g., of persons like Carothers at Du Pont which led to nylon, or Shockley's work which led to the transistor, in the earlier cases the scientific research that created the breakthrough was completely autonomous to the inventive effort, while in the latter cases much of the scientific knowledge was won in the course of efforts specifically aimed at providing the basic understanding needed to further technological advances. Carothers' basic research at Du Pont which led to nylon was financed by management in the hope that improvments in the understanding of long polymers would lead to important or new improved chemical processes, and nylon came as a byproduct of this. Shockley's work, e.g., on transistors, which came at Bell Telephone Laboratories project, was undertaken in the belief that improved knowledge of semiconductors would lead to better electrical devices.

The new industries of the 1970s and the 1980s—the polymers and plastics, electronics and optics, chemicals and synthetics, cryogenics and fluidics, aerospace and communications—and such dramatic products as computers, lasers, and holograms are all integrally science based. They can develop only to the extent that there is a broad advance in basic scientific knowledge in these fields.

Science-based industries and technologies have a distinct advantage in achieving major advances in products and processes. Instead of chance development, or the classic inventive effort of direct attack on a problem, products in these industries emerge out of linked, systematic research and reflect the maturing of the science base in these industries. As Nelson, Peck, and Kalacheck point out: many of the products of the science-based industries are materials used by other industries. This has led to rapid productivity growth in many sectors of the economy. The more important new consumer goods have come either directly from these industries or through incorporation into new products by other industries which are created by the science-based sector.

If one thinks broadly of the major factors which will affect the development of every advanced economy in the next several decades, the three major ones would be: industry size, advances in science and education, and the development of a scientific base under the technology of an industry.

The Role of Technological Forecasting

If the development of science-based industries is the heart of a post-industrial society, linked to this is the necessity of technological forecasting. Technology inevitably introduces an uncertainty to the economy. The development of new products and new industries can mean the complete displacement of previous industries with woe befalling the companies—and the regions— which had been associated with these. New technologies provide vastly different requirements in the needs of capital and manpower. Just as some degree of economic forecasting is necessary to smooth out the ups and downs of the business cycle, so some degree of technological forecasting is necessary to introduce stability in the control of social change.

Most technological forecasting is still made on the basis of what an imaginative engineer or writer can dream up as possible. In 1892, a German engineer named Plessner forecast technological developments (supercritical steam and metal vapor turbines) and some functional capabilities (such as television and voice-operated typewriters) which were—and to some extent still are—far in the future. Arthur C. Clarke, who has made some of the more speculative forecasts in his serious science fiction (e.g., international telecommunications) has argued that anything that is theoretically possible will be achieved, despite technical difficulties, if it is desired greatly enough. That, however, may be an ideal speculation. "Fantastic" ideas, he says, have been achieved in the past, and only by assuming that they will continue to be achieved do we have any hope of anticipating the future. Much of this kind of expectation is "poetry," because little attention is paid to constraints, especially economic ones. Fantasy may be indispensable, but only if it is disciplined by technique. Marshall McLuhan, with his usual gift for paradox, has said that the improvement of intuition is a highly technical matter.

Within the next decades, we may expect to see systematic technological forecasting. In recent years a variety of techniques have been developed. These include "envelope curve" techniques, the morphological matrices of Fritz Zwicky, the "relevance trees," and similar techniques.[4] Much of the early impetus to disciplined technological forecasting was pioneered by the remarkable man Theodor von Karman, the eminent scientist from the California Institute of Technology in the field of aerodynamics. His report in 1944 on the future of aircraft propulsion is the first modern technological forecast. Von Karman later initiated the concentrated technological forecasting, at five-year intervals, of the U.S. Air Force and the technological forecasting in NATO. His innovations were fairly simple. Von Karman did not try to predict a specific product—one could not do that. He looked at basic potentialities and limitations, at functional capabilities and key parameters, rather than

try to describe in particular terms the detailed technological products of the future. He emphasized the evalu-
ation of alternative combinations of future basic technologies, and he sought to place his forecasts in a
well-defined time frame of fifteen to twenty years.

It may be useful, at this point, to indicate some of
the basic technological developments that one can try to
foresee in the next twenty to thirty years with a special
concentration for this audience on those which will affect
international relations and international strength, and
seek to draw some of the economic consequences from
them.

The Technology of the 1970s and 1980s

One of the major changes in the nature of advanced
industrial societies is the increasing independence of
these economies from raw-material location and sources
of energy as the limiting factors in their ability to develop. In the past every society had to live integrally near
its basic raw-material resources and use its energy
sources. Chemistry, which as I have pointed out is the
first "modern" industry, allows one to create synthetics
from a variety of easily available primary products and
either to substitute for raw materials (such as synthetic
rubber for natural rubber), or to compete with a whole
variety of natural or fabricated products (e.g., plastics for
wood, glass, aluminum, or steel). Thus one becomes
freed of certain kinds of immediate raw material resources for synthetic fabrication. Striking reductions of
costs in transportation (such as the large oil tankers,
which offset previous travel shortcuts such as the Suez
Canal, or large speedy freighters) have extended the

range of movement of bulk energy sources such as oil and coal. The most striking example of this new independence from raw-material energy sources is the postwar development of the steel industry in Japan. Japan imports 88 per cent of her iron ore and 64 per cent of her coking coal at an average distance of 5,500 miles. Yet Japan today is the third largest steel producer in the world, after the United States and the Soviet Union. In short, it is the nature of superior technology which is the principal factor in the strength of industrial societies.[5]

If one looks ahead two decades, there are five major international developments in technology which will affect the relative strength of nations.[6] These are:

1. Changes in the Nature of Energy Production.

Progress in this area includes fast breeder reactors, controlled thermonuclear reaction, superconductivity and magnetohydrodynamics (MHD). The cost of energy, utilizing these processes, is likely to come down sharply in the next two decades, and nations with these capabilities will be in a position to manufacture cheaper products for competition. Controlled thermonuclear reaction would lead to single reactors with as much generating capacity—10,000 megawatts—as the total capacity of Poland in 1967, and increasingly less a dependence simply upon raw-material resources. Superconductors, through the use of pure metals, result in the nearly complete elimination of resistance in the transmission of electric current. MHD, using superheated gases through a magnetic field, would provide for more than 25 per cent electric power from a given amount of thermal energy. And these are quite realistic possibilities for, let us say, the next twenty years.

2. The Spread of International Telecommunications Through Global Satellites.

The drop in telecommunications costs—by 1980, it may be possible to make a call anywhere in the world for $1.00—will speed the flow of international business. A global TV network is a distinct technological possibility. Television has already had the effect of making countries "national societies" in that events taking place in one section have an immediate repercussion in all others. One can see this in the "contagion effects" of the race situation in the United States. The war in Vietnam has been made immediately vivid by the fast relay of news pictures through international satellites. What will happen when the idea of "one world" becomes a communications reality?

3. The Development of Marine Resources.

The extraction of energy sources, particularly oil and natural gas, from below the seabed has begun to expand rapidly—present annual revenues of offshore oil now exceeds $7 billion—and underwater exploration at depths between 500 and 1,000 feet may take place in this decade, and more extensive engineering operations in the next. Besides oil and gas, there are indications of metal resources which can be mined, and other mineral sources, under the sea.

4. The Use of Earth Resource Satellites for Exploration.

Sometime in the 1970s, the U.S. National Aeronautics and Space Administration (NASA) is expected to launch an "earth resources technology satellite" and it hopes to have an operational system by the end of the decade. Using various sensor devices (heat waves, optical devices, sound waves, etc.), the satellite is expected to "map" mineral sources in the world (and uncover sources in relatively unexplored, out-of-the-way geographical regions); chart the coverage of snow, sand, and vegetation distribution, and thus help in the planning of irrigation and power and the control of floods; map the ocean currents and temperatures, and the like. Through the satellite, NASA hopes to provide a basic inventory of information of the distribution of natural resources and natural processes of the earth.

5. The Prediction and Possible Control of Weather.

In the next decade, we are likely to see more successful prediction of weather, through information gathered by satellites, and equally through the "modeling" and "simulation" of weather movements. In the next two decades we are likely to see the control of weather through cloud seeding and various devices which will direct the drop in rainfall. As a further possibility, we may yet see the large-scale modification of climate through major changes in the pattern of currents.

Fifteen years ago, the great mathematician and scientist, John von Neumann, speculated that large-scale changes in climate could be created by use of "microscopic layers of colored matter" on large ice fields, which would allow them to absorb the heat of the sun, and the melting of the ice of Greenland and Antartica could produce worldwide tropical and semitropical climate.[7] More recently, a Russian scientist, P. M. Borisov, has speculated that if the Bering Strait were dammed, and the lesser saline waters of the Artic Ocean were pumped out, one could change the character of the Gulf Stream and change the climate of northern Siberia, Alaska, and northern Canada.[8]

These are rather fanciful speculations, and probably far out of the range of existing technological, let alone economic capacities. But the more limited aspects of weather prediction and rainfall control are important aspects affecting the economy of every nation of the world.

If one looks at these possible technological developments alone, there are three major socioeconomic consequences that one can project that will become fateful in the next decades.

Of these three possible technological developments, one is the fact that the developments outlined are huge and costly, and can be undertaken only on a giant scale. The change of scale has been one of the marked features of a modern society, both in the size of enterprises and the nature of markets. Large economies of scale require enormous capital sums and resources for their effects to be realized. Even in such "conventional" items as transformers for power networks, as Victor Basiuk points out, the minimum economic size of a plant needed to produce the huge transformers necessary to take advantage of the economies of scale is pushing producers into cooperation or mergers. Today, e.g., most European companies are incapable of producing the huge transformers needed for the continuously increasing voltage in the networks. In the United States, five producers supply the entire market, while in Europe there are as many as thirty.

Thus the nature of these new technology developments, particularly in energy resources, force by the change of scale a movement toward consolidation and merger. Secondly, the nature of modern joint technology is becoming a compelling reason for economic integration either within regional groupings of countries, or even worldwide, as in the case of telecommunications. Great Britain and France have had to come together to develop a supersonic transport. Electric power grids tie together West European countries in order to rationalize the use of a large-scale generating capacity. Power exchanges are taking place between Canada and the United States, and facilities now under construction in Paraguay in South America will be shared with neighboring Brazil and Argentina. "It is entirely possible," writes Lester Brown, "that we will someday see a worldwide electrical power grid permitting the system to balance high daytime requirements on one side of the globe with low nighttime requirements of the other side, thus permitting vast savings."[9]

And thirdly, the forthcoming technological changes in weather control, as well as the distribution of worldwide communication channels, necessarily fosters more international cooperation in order to distribute the information, share in the results, and regulate the needs. In monetary policy, communication, transportation, fishing rights, patents, ocean exploration, and to a more limited extent international trade, we already have supra-national agencies which have assumed various responsibilities of government. These are likely to spread in the next two decades.

One major new factor of the last decade will spur the demand for international economic regulation. This is the tremendous growth of the multinational corporation. Of the fifty largest economic entities in the world, thirty-seven are countries and thirteen are corporations.[10] Of the top one hundred, fifty-one are corporations. The larger or global corporations for the most part have their headquarters within the United States. Of the top ten multinational firms, eight are American, the other two European. Of the top fifty multinational corporations, thirty-nine are U.S. based. The foreign output of U.S.-based multinational firms already amounts to a "third world economy" with estimates ranging between $120 billion to $200 billion a year.

The multinational corporation is primarily a response to these changes in technology and markets in terms of scale and integration. If one looks at these changes through the prism of imperialism and empire— I use the words in a descriptive sense in that any major power invariably seeks to enlarge its hegemony and domination—then the U.S.-based global corporation is an aspect, too, of the post-industrial society. In the early nineteenth century, where primary products and raw materials were the chief staples of trade, the pattern of trade and imperialism was an emphasis, largely, on product markets in which the advanced economies bought primary products and exported manufactured goods. In the second, classic phase of imperialism (as described by Hobson and Hilferding, and adapted by Lenin), the relationships between advanced economies and primary producers rested largely on the export of capital and investment in these underdeveloped countries. But in the post-industrial society, there is a different set of relationships in which the "export" is chiefly advanced technology and organizational capability. It is for this reason that, increasingly in the last decade, the United States, as an emergent post-industrial society, has forged its economic relationships primarily with Europe, as a market for these capacities, rather than with Africa or Asia.[11]

In these changed economic relationships, the global corporation begins to assume an economic power and to formulate economic policies which can seriously affect the policies of many of the nation-states. Where a single corporation or a group of corporations command more production resources than the state, such a power can frustrate national objectives. The political and economic relationships between the global corporations and the national states will be one of the major questions to be worked out in the next decade or two.

Let me turn briefly to some social problems of the post-industrial society. The concept of a post-industrial society, as I have said, deals primarily with long-run structural changes in the society. It is not, nor can it be, as I have indicated, a comprehensive model of the complete society itself. It does not deal with basic changes in values (such as the hedonism which now legitimates the spending patterns of an affluent society); it can say little about the nature of political crises, such as the U.S. entrapment in Vietnam or the racial disorders which have erupted in recent years; it cannot assess the quality of the national "will" which is so important in the immediate political decisions of a society. However, by positing certain fundamental shifts in the bases of class position and in modes of access to places in the society, and by introducing a new crucial variable, that of "the centrality of theoretical knowledge," it does outline certain problems which a society must now solve. Just as an industrial society has been organized politically and culturally in diverse ways by the U.S.S.R., Germany, and Japan, so too the post-industrial society may have diverse political and cultural forms. The character of that society, however, will be shaped by specific political decisions.

The most crucial questions that will be faced by every postindustrial society will deal with education, talent, and science policy. The rapid expansion of a professional and technical class, and the increased dependence of the society on scientific manpower, suggest a new and absolute unique dimension in social affairs: i.e., that the economic growth rate of a postindustrial society will be less dependent on money capital than on "human capital." And this poses many new problems in the way of planning. In the past (and in many of the less-developed countries today), societies stepping onto the escalator of industrialization required huge sums of money capital to develop the economic infrastructure (highways, railroads, canals), necessary for transportation and communication, and for the basic physical plant of heavy industry. Tomorrow, however, the long-range economic expansion of the society will be limited by shortages in technical and scientific manpower. Such problems are novel. We know from economic theory how to raise money capital—we restrict consumption and use the resultant savings for investment—even though the political mechanisms are not easy to manipulate. But the source of brainpower is limited in part by the genetic distributions of talent and also by cultural disadvantages. The process of identifying and husbanding talent is long and difficult, and it involves the provision of adequate motivation, proper counselling and guidance, a coherent curriculum, and the like. The "time-cycle" in such planning—a period of from fifteen to twenty years—is vastly different from that required in the raising of money capital.

The nature of education itself is bound to change; it will necessarily become a continuing, lifetime affair for the professional and technical person. Beyond the colleges and graduate schools we will need postdoctoral universities where new knowledge and new techniques can be passed along. Such continuing pressures and ratings inevitably invite increased anxiety. For many persons, the achievement of college was equivalent to reaching a plateau, to "having it made." It was a guarantee of higher pay and a higher status in society. With the erosion of that system, with the plateau becoming more of a slope, more psychological strains will be introduced into society.

In the post-industrial society, the university necessarily achieves a new, central role. It is the place where theoretical knowledge is sought, tested, and codified in a disinterested way, and thus it becomes the source of new knowledge and innovation. It has a new importance as the gatekeeper for the society. With the increasing "professionalization" of occupations, the university becomes the source of all training. Outside the classic professions, one went to a university for a liberal education and then learned "on the job." With old knowledge becoming quickly obsolete, the greater need is a grounding in theory, and only in the university can one acquire the conceptual structures that allow one to organize and reorganize new knowledge for the purpose of instrumental use. Perhaps it is not too much to say that just as the business firm was the key institution of the past hundred and fifty years, the research institution, because of its new role as the source of innovation, will become the primary institution in the next fifty years.

The chief question is whether the university is sufficiently adaptive and flexible to undertake the vast new functions that are being thrust upon it so rapidly. In the past, and to some extent in the present, the ideal of the university saw it as the place for humane learning, for maintaining a relation to tradition. Under the weight of the new professional demands, the liberal-arts tradition and the function may crumble—to the disadvantage of society. The multiplicity of new demands—for research, for application, for consultation, for training of graduate students, for the custodial and experimental work on government and large science projects—may itself become so huge a burden that a different system, dividing many of the functions between universities and new social forms may be necessary.

The post-industrial society involves the extension of a particular kind of rationality associated largely with science, technology, and economics. When applied to politics, this rationality becomes technocratic, and inevitably it creates a populist reaction. But the most violent reaction to the new rationality is in the culture.

The most diffuse, but in the long run the most potentially disintegrating force in the society is a new kind of sensibility in American culture. The relationship between social structure and culture is perhaps the most complicated of all problems of social analysis. A change in the economy or in technology is constrained by resources and costs. One cannot introduce a new product or a new machine until one knows that one can absorb this cost or one has the resources. Such changes have had a determinable time sequence in a society. But changes in culture, in expressive symbols and values, in statements about the meaning of experience, and in the codes for the guidance of behavior—the dimensions of art and imagination—are unconstrained. At times, as Ortega has said, they foreshadow the social reality of tomorrow because they are played out in the mind; but at times they remain only in the imagination. Thus it is difficult to specify the exact consequences of experiments in sensibility which go on all around us. Some do anticipate tomorrow, some can exhaust themselves very quickly.

The important fact is that for the last hundred years the culture of the Western intelligentsia has been largely anti-institutional and even antinomian. In the celebration of the self and the individual, valuable as these are, it presented a polarity of the individual versus society. It exalted the idea of the genius, or the artist, above societal convention. But today everybody regards themselves, perhaps as part of the democratization of genius, as individualistic, and very many people are therefore waiting for a chance to break out of the forms of social conventions. The idea stresses therefore that self-expression and self-fulfillment are open to all without regard for boundaries and limits. In the "cult of experience" all realms of experience must be open and explored. While this affords us a very rich and often entrancing basis for exploration, it also means that everything is under attack: authority, because no man is better than any other; the past, because learning tells us nothing; discipline and specialization, because they presumably constrict experience.

Primarily, what has been added to the anti-intellectualism and anti-nomianism of the past is a form of anti-institutionalism and anti-rationality. What is celebrated is expression rather than idea, improvisation rather than text, sincerity rather than judgment. The psychedelic experience and the drug culture, the search for the "high" and for extended awareness, are the mass manifestations of this phenomenon. In this fierce anti-intellectualism, feeling and sentiment, not thought, are considered more important. Education becomes not the transmission of learning, but a search for "meaningful identity" to be gained by "dialogue," "encounter" and "confrontation."

This has been tried in many respects to political issues but as these political issues recede, it is likely that the cultural radicalism, which preceded the political and has deeper roots in the past will be extended. The cultist aspects of these movements may fade from fashion, but it would be a mistake to assume that the deeper impulses will pass. For the time being, all this is restricted to a small number, yet they are the culture-bearers of an age.

Any culture movement is multifaceted, and some interesting new areas of creativity will probably emerge from this new sensibility. But the *social* question is not the character of a new kind of high culture, but the fact that, for the first time, a sensibility of this kind has permeated a larger mass which by itself is not creative, yet which presumes that its experience, its search for "the true self" is as relevant as all art, and is in that respect becoming, it seems to me, a social problem for any society.

In the end there is the beginning, as T. S. Eliot wrote, and we return to the question that is the root of all political philosophy: What is the good life that one wants to lead? The politics of the future—for those who operate at least within the society—will not be quarrels between functional economic-interest groups for distributive shares of the national product, but necessarily the concerns of communal society, particularly the inclusion of disadvantaged groups. These problems will turn on the issues of instilling a responsible social ethos in our leaders, the demand for more amenities, for greater beauty and a better quality of life in the arrangement of our cities, a more differentiated and intellectual educational system, and an improvement in the character of our culture. We may be divided on how to achieve these aims, and how to apportion the costs. But such questions, deriving from a conception of public virtue, bring us back to the fundamental questions asked by the classical *polis*. And this is as it should be.

Note: This essay was written three years ago. The major dimensional lack is political forecasting. And as I have argued (in *Towards the Year 2000*) political forecasting is inherently more difficult than any other, yet politics affects our lives more than other factors. This discussion, then, has to be read in the light of a caveat: it is not a prediction of "the future," but a set of speculations within a limited frame.—D.B.

Notes

The Post Industrial Society—Expectations for the 1970s and 1980s *(Bell)*

1. Paul Valéry, *Reflections on the World Today* (New York: Pantheon Books, 1948), p. 16.
2. "The US Economy in 1980: a preview of BLS projections," *Monthly Labor Review* (April 1970).
3. Nelson, Peck, and Kalachek, *Technology, Economic Growth and Public Policy* (Washington, D.C., 1967), p. 41.
4. For a detailed analysis, see Erich Jantsch, *Technological Forecasting in Perspective* (Paris: O.E.C.D., 1967).
5. I am indebted here to Victor Basiuk, research associate of the Institute of Science in Human Affairs at Columbia University for materials.
6. I leave aside here developments within particular industries such as polymers and electronics, and the vast area of biomedical technology. The choice here is dictated by an examination of international impacts.
7. See John von Neumann, "Can We Survive Technology," in *The Fabulous Future: America in 1980,* ed. by the Editors of *Fortune* (New York, 1966), p. 41.
8. P. M. Borisov, "Can We Control the Arctic Climate?" Bulletin of the Atomic Scientists (March 1969).
9. Lester Brown, "The Nation State, The Multinational Corporation and the Changing World Order." Paper prepared for the Commission on the Year 2000, American Academy of Arts and Sciences.
10. The largest firms, in rank order, are General Motors, Ford Motor, Standard Oil of New Jersey, Royal Dutch/-Shell, General Electric, Chrysler, Unilever, Mobil Oil,

45

Texaco, U.S. Steel, I.B.M., Gulf Oil, and Western Electric. General Motors has an annual product of $20.2 billion, which puts it thirteenth in a world ranking of size of annual product, just behind Mexico ($20.7 billion), Australia ($21.9), and Brazil, which is number ten, with $22.7 billion. The figures are from Lester Brown, *ibid.*

11. *The Wall Street Journal* of July 10, 1969, notes that the Ford Motor Company is Britain's biggest exporter, while I.B.M. dominates France's computer and office-equipment exports.

PETER F. DRUCKER, born in Vienna in 1909, received his education there and in England. His doctorate in public and international law is from Frankfurt University in Germany. He is Professor of Management at the Graduate Business School of New York University, and Clarke Professor of Social Science at Claremont Graduate School in Claremont, California.

Dr. Drucker is a management consultant, specializing in business and economic policy and in top management organization. He has advised several of the largest companies in the United States as well as leading companies in Europe and elsewhere; agencies of the U.S. Government and several governments such as those of Canada and Japan; public-service institutions such as universities and hospitals.

Among his books are *The New Society* (1950), *The Practice of Management* (1954), *America's Next Twenty Years* (1957), *The Landmarks of Tomorrow* (1960), *Managing for Results* (1964), *The Effective Executive* (1967), *The Age of Discontinuity* (1969), *Technology, Management and Society* (1970), and *Men, Ideas, and Politics* (1971).

Management's New Role—
The Price of Success
PETER F. DRUCKER

Many thinkers have analyzed "society today and tomorrow" in very broad context. Others have considered a much narrower focus. On the work of the manager, my task is to be a bridge between the two. I have to set the manager's role into a broad social context. I shall try to sketch out some of the new challenges, new opportunities and new tasks which managers and especially business managers will face in the kind of society our friends and colleagues have presented for us.

Perhaps the best way to start is to say that management has been the success story of a century which has not been one of the most successful centuries in human history. It has been the success story as a new function, as a new discipline, and as a new leadership group in society. To the emergence of management, which dates back to the early days of the century, we owe the achievements in large measure of this century—achievements which are not primarily scientific but primarily social and economic achievements. We owe to management the success of the material civilization which, for the first time in the history of man, has made it possible not only to dream of, but more important, to work on, eliminating poverty as a natural condition of man. How successful management has been one can see by contrasting it with what Ota Sik called the "conflict between the capital and the wage fund" behind the Iron Curtain and the need to make owners out of the wage earners. In the advanced countries of the West this is accomplished fact. Only we have found perhaps a financially more attractive solution than the one he gave us. In Sweden 35 per cent or so of the ownership of the larger companies is held by the wage earners through mutual funds, pension funds, insurance companies. In the United States the figure is closer to 60 per cent. If the present trends continue— and in view of the age structure of the population, they will continue—Sweden will have 50 per cent of the ownership of its privately owned business in the hands of trustees of the employees. That, believe me, is a better way of accomplishing the socialization of property than to have the coal miners own 70 per cent of the coal mines or of any other declining business. As an old financial man I know that it is not sound for anybody to have his assets in only one investment.

So we have a material achievement which for the first time makes possible not only the abolition of poverty but the abolition of the old conflicts between various factors of production. Even more important is the achievement in building organizations which are the only reason why Herman Kahn and Daniel Bell can talk about the need for educated people. Educated people do not make their living by themselves, they make them as members of an organization. There is very little that is less productive than one of today's educated people out by himself, because he is a specialist. We owe it to the organization that the great mass of people today can acquire a learning and an education that goes far beyond anything which anybody could have dreamed of a few generations ago. In the population of my grandfather's day perhaps one-tenth of one per cent could possibly spend all these years in school. We also have learned in the last twenty years that management is the one hope we have for economic and social development. If we have learned one thing, it is that capital does not develop. Capital by itself only creates a liability. Unless you have the human resources, the managerial resources to make capital multiply and be really effective you get no development no matter how much capital you pour in. What a very brilliant South American said of his continent, namely "Latin America is not underdeveloped, it is undermanaged," applies to all underdeveloped and developing countries I know.

But if one learns one thing from the history of man, it is that every achievement has a price. We have a saying in America, "There ain't no free lunch." Believe me, there is no free lunch. One always pays for it, one way or another.

Every achievement has its price; and a very great achievement exacts a very great price. The price of success for management therefore will be very high and we are going to have to pay it in the next ten to fifteen years. We will be expected—as a result of our success—to give leadership and direction in the major problems that face the community: the preservation of our physical environment, the restoration of our capacity to have communities and the maintenance of political cohesion where the world's economy is increasingly, truly worldwide, while the world political system is still parochial, still in very small units, and increasingly fragmented. There is no tendency in this century toward political unification. All the tendencies in this century, beginning with the dissolution of the union between Sweden and Norway, have been toward political fragmentation. The last act of union was the incorporation of the Boer republics into the British Empire in 1900. Since then we have seen only fragmentation and I see no reason to believe that the process has run its course. And yet we clearly need a world unity, and so far the only sphere in which there are even the slightest traces of it is the economic one, and that is a managerial achievement.

In this century our society has changed fundamentally. In fact it is very hard for us to imagine how great the change has been. In 1900 or so, if you had looked around, the world would have looked very flat indeed. As the highest building you would have seen a churchspire on the horizon—the central government. It would have looked very big, but I do not know whether you realize how small it really was. Perhaps one needs to realize that the small Israeli army three years ago had more firepower than all the armies in World War I had together. Perhaps one needs to realize that all the ministries of any government any place in the world in 1900 could easily have found office space in one modern ministry building, and there would have been room to spare for a grand opera and a skating rink. Perhaps one needs to realize that the largest university of 1900—which was Tokyo— had fewer than 5,000 students. Berlin came next. In both countries the legislatures at that time were so concerned over this giant monstrosity that bills were proposed in both parliaments to split off parts of the universities. The Germans actually succeeded—they split off pure-science research. I have been in and out of universities for almost forty years, and let me say, I have seen nothing that makes me doubt the wisdom of those parlamentarians of seventy years ago. Indeed a university of 28,000–40,000 students *is* a monstrosity and unmanageable and I think we will have to dismember it. I think 5,000 students make more sense.

In 1900 the hospital was the place where the poor went to die. My doctor uncle went to the hospital one morning a week out of the kindness of his heart; but he would never have put one of his own patients there. Respectable people did not go to the hospital—the poor went there to die. The hospital was small and had about two menial workers for each five patients or ten patients; today the hospital is the health center of the community and has about four to five employees for each patient. In 1900 the world was essentially a world of molecular diffusion in which the one really effective social unit was the family. The government was there but it was very limited. Today you have a world in which every single social task is being performed in and through a giant organization that has to be managed. Whether you talk of the armed forces or of the government agency or of the university or of the hospital or the business, they are all large institutions. This is one of the things the young people today see very clearly. That the world has become institutionalized is one of the things they see very, very clearly. I am not going to reflect on the desirability of this change. I am simply saying it has happened.

Let me only as an aside say that this had a lot to do

with the problems of the family. Today the problem of the family is not that it has become less important to the young people, but that it has become infinitely more important. The problem is that they put an emotional burden on the family which families bluntly are not equipped to handle. If you read any Victorian diary, you will find that families were not centers of love and affection, but centers of hatred, dissension, quarrelling, and contempt. But they were necessary. It did you no good to fight with your brother, hate your father, and despise your children. You had to stick with them for sheer survival. The family was the only unit of effective social action, whether it was taking care of the old and the sick or supporting the orphan nieces and nephews or finding somebody a job. When I started to work over forty years ago, the only way to find a job was still through an uncle who knew an uncle who knew an uncle; there were no placement offices, there were no employment offices. The family did all this. The family in an age in which very few people went to school much beyond the age of twelve or so, was also the main focus of learning, whether the learning was out of books or whether it was an apprenticeship. Today every one of these functions is being discharged by a massive social agency of one kind or another. The family was also the center of production in a world in which 60–70 per cent of the people—or 80 per cent—still either lived on the land or made their living as small craftsmen, that is, in family enterprises. Today that is being done increasingly by highly organized economic institutions. So the family is no longer needed for physical survival. But it is still needed for emotional survival. Therefore, you see the tremendous burden the young people place on the family; the demands they are making on their parents are totally unrealistic. You may have heard that in May 1971 four students were killed in a riot at an American Midwestern university. Those "student rebels," out to riot against the "Establishment," the night before had each called home and talked to their parents and had assured them that they would not go out the next day. Well, nineteen-year-olds do not always do what they tell their parents. But when we were nineteen, it would not have occurred to us to consult our parents. We would have spurned that. No member of my generation would have considered his parents relevant in such a matter. This is a very small symptom of a change in the demands the young make, and the closeness to their parents they want. And of course the expectation of the perfection and perfectability of parents is totally unrealistic. But the family is not dissolving, it is cohering. It is becoming very much tighter than it has ever been before, precisely because it is no longer a physical- and social-survival need; it is an emotional and human one.

But I don't want to talk about the family today. I am supposed to talk about management. The family one hundred years ago was our only social institution, but a totally incompetent social institution. It could not do anything. It is unbelievable how incompetent historical society was at handling what we would consider the simplest problems. Nobody knew what to do, and if anybody knew what to do there was no means of doing it. We then developed special-purpose institutions, each highly specialized, to accomplish this or that task. There is business charged with the task of producing and distributing economic goods and services, and the school system and the university system and the government agencies, and the health-care center, the hospital, and the medical practice and so on—each of them highly competent in one specialized area and our society owes its performance capacity to this development of specialized institutions.

We have applied the old principle of the specialization of labor to the needs of society, for beyond its old application to the needs of production and distribution. As a result we can now do things that were simply unheard of even fifty to sixty years ago. But we have, if I may use an analogy, a lot of first-rate virtuosos without a conductor and without a score, each improvising his own tune, and as a result we have no community institution. We have a society in which single tasks are done superbly, but in which there is nobody who is really concerned with the whole or able to see the whole.

You may say "What about the government?" and you heard me right. One of the basic changes is the increasing incompetence of government to be anything but a series of special-purpose institutions, and so there is the increasing incompetence of government to govern. Small countries do not suffer from this as much as the large ones, and in that respect it is a distinct advantage to be a small country today. Large countries, and I am not talking of giants only, are in effect becoming ungovernable. No government has control, let alone is capable of giving direction. Above all, no government can any longer control its own bureaucracy, which goes on doing what it wants to do, no matter what the political leadership says. Most of the time they do a good job, but they only do a very limited job. They try to make the world safe for social security or for irrigation. They do that very well. But they, too, do not see the community. They see their own very narrow specialty.

We have a pluralistic society again. This is something new and it is something that the sociologists do not see, since they do not look at all of society, only at individual institutions. We have a pluralistic society again, while our theory and our practice in the West has assumed a unitary society for three hundred years. We again have a society in which there are major power centers, diffused, not one of them concerned with the whole. We have again a fragmented society rather like the one unmade when the baroque state overthrew the mighty barons. We have again a pluralistic society, but it is very different from any pluralist society we have ever known in history. The pluralism which the Renaissance and the early modern ages destroyed was a horizontal pluralism in which there were bigger and smaller units, but in which essentially everybody from duke and baron to yeoman did the same things and was concerned with the same matters. Everybody, in fact, was concerned with wresting a living from the land. Everybody knew what the other units were doing. The only difference between them was in size and scope and power. Today's organizations do different things and they do not rank each other. The duke ranked the count. But it would be foolish to say that the university ranks the government agency or that the business ranks the hospital. In the society which our history books describe everybody worried constantly about rank and precedence. If you read memoirs of the court of Louis XIV you find that that was all everybody cared about: who went first through the door, who sat down first at the table, who was allowed to wear three ermine tails instead of two. Nobody today worries about precedence in that sense between various institutions. What all these managers worry about is something quite different, something our ancestors never worried about, namely communications. They worry about talking to each other. There was no problem of that kind four hundred years ago; everybody understood everybody because they all had the same concerns. But today these special-purpose institutions see the world from the point of view of their special tasks and that is all they see. And so they worry, and rightly, about communications, but they do not worry about rank.

The government may indeed still be the top institution, but I am beginning to have my doubts. At most it is only the chairman, the first among equals in a way. These institutions are autonomous in the sense that their task has to be done and that it has to be done under its own rationale. Dr. Sik has maintained that a political system that is unwilling to accept the autonomy of the economic task will not get the economic task done. Exactly the same may be said about the university or about the hospital. Therefore, these are autonomous institutions which in effect cannot be controlled by politics. All that government can do is squabble about the budget, but all of us know ways of getting the money we need some way or other. I am very worried about the decline of government, not in its size but in its performance capacity.

So we have a new society in its hard crystal structure, and it is a pluralism that differs from any we have ever heard of in history, a pluralism for which we have neither political nor social theory. But that does not bother me greatly. One thing one learns is that philosophy comes at the end of historial development. Philosophers codify the past; till then they cannot function. So if we do not have them today, it simply means that the task is ahead of us. You will not get any help from them now, because that is not their function. Their function is to tell us a hundred years later what we have already done. But the task is here and now. And nobody is in charge of the community. If you go back to the pluralism of old, every one of these terribly incompetent units was a total community in the sense that whatever was done in the community was done in and through them. In fact they drew no distinction between private business and public business, between family affairs and education. All were community affairs. Each was a total community, from the small household of the yeoman farmer all the way up to the mighty duke to the king. Today we have special-purpose institutions, but we have none that is concerned with the whole community. What we need is not conformity, but diversity. This is, I think, the lesson of totalitarian regimes in this century which are above all an example of inability to perform anything except to wage war and depreciate the currency. We do not need mechanism but we need organic autonomy. We do not need dictation, but we need self-direction and self-control. The young people are right in saying that we do not need more authority, we need more responsibility. This is the most necessary task.

This task is particularly a challenge to economic managers, that is, to business leaders, for a number of reasons. They may not strike us as particularly good reasons, but there is no point in arguing with reality. They are the reasons why the community is looking to us and will continue to look to us. The first reason why the community expects a business manager in the developed countries to take leadership is simply that he has already performed well. You may say this is very peculiar, because in every developed country you find bitter criticism of business when you conduct a public-opinion poll. But when you look at what business is criticized for, it is criticized for not being perfect. The expectations are unbelievably high, they are much too high; and when you ask young people not "Do you like business?" but "From whom do you expect answers to these problems?" you will find again and again and again that business ranks first because it performs. Businessmen are the only ones who have effectively performed. This is so obvious to everybody that it does not occur to them that there may be limitations on what we can do.

The second reason is simply that business has measurements. A market economy provides measurements. Above all in a market economy one can go bankrupt if one does not perform. No other institution has any real measurements of performance. No other one has even coherent measurements of costs, let alone of results. In part, this is because it is very hard to define the objectives of, let us say, a hospital, a school system, or a government. If you cannot set objectives, you cannot measure; there is no market test. Therefore, the only measurements we have are our economic measurements which are not strictly applicable to the other institutions. One of the basic problems, therefore, is that one never knows whether they perform or not until it is much too late to do anything about it. So we look to the one institution that has measurements, where one can say: they are doing their job reasonably well and are allocating resources to results, or, they are doing it poorly and are depriving society and economy of the benefit of resources.

The third reason is that business, so far, is the only institution capable of being multinational—and I am not an uncritical admirer of the multinational companies. I work with far too many of them not to see the problems and their limitations. (By the way, Sweden is number two in the multinational parade. The United States is number one. But in relation to gross national product Sweden has a larger proportion of Swedish-owned production outside the national territory than any other country.) L. M. Ericsson or ASEA or General Electric or Westinghouse are the only institutions that can and do look at a larger economy and technology, as Herman Kahn, Daniel Bell, and Dr. Segerstedt have pointed out. The nation is too small a unit to make rational economic decisions, indeed to make optimal economic decisions even for the nation. One has at least to do what our Japanese friends are doing: they are exceedingly nationalistic in the best sense and the worst sense of the word, but they start out considering the world economy before they make a domestic national decision. That is one of the secrets of their tremendous success and growth. The multinational company is the only institution that can transfer the needed development skills today, which are social skills, not technical skills. It is the only institution that can view the world economy or at least a big economy, and is the only institution capable of bringing together people from various nationalities in a common task. In an age of rampant nationalism this is no mean achievement. It is a very difficult achievement and by no means done well, but at least it is being attempted there, and nobody else is trying.

Finally we have a discipline of management. We do not know very much about it, but we do know a little bit. We are a little beyond the doctors of Molière's time. Occasionally a patient survives. We are a little bit beyond them and maybe not enough. But at least we have the beginnings of a rational discipline that can be learned. (I am not saying one can teach it. I have been trying to do so for twenty years and I am not sure one can. But one can learn management.) The rational discipline of management is not yet very good; it is primitive. I think our grandchildren will laugh at most of the things we believe to be true. But at least we have the beginning. So we are, so to speak, elected to give leadership, whether we like it or not. These factors explain something that has been puzzling me and a good many other people: the "management boom" of the last twenty years. I will give you one example. When the Canadians unified their armed services a few years ago and merged their army, navy, and air force into one military service, they called a preliminary conference of generals and admirals. What was the topic of that first conference?—not strategy, not careers, not training of young officers. It was management. I am not sure they were well advised; but that is not the point. The point is that management was the obvious choice to all of them as the first topic of concern for the unified services. This is very typical. This "management boom" means that the other institutions are coming to us and saying: What can we learn from you?

I do not teach young people. I teach adults with eight or ten years of experience and in my classes the last twenty years I have had at least as many managers from public-service institutions as I have had business managers. I think there is not a hospital or school administrator in New York who has not been to one of our classes (not necessarily mine). I am not saying that they are learning anything, I am saying they are coming and coming back not because we are so good, but because they are so bad. We don't have much, but they have nothing. They only have procedures. What passes for public administration in most cases is a squabble over how many carbon copies you want to make and the answer is: get a duplicating machine and stop worrying about it. By and large that is the essence of public administration. It is procedural matters; and the same is true of what passes for administrative knowledge in other areas. If you want to talk of objectives or planning or allocation of resources or even such simple things as personnel policy and human relations, you have to go to business management, not because we are very good, but because the others are so much worse. So management is expected to take the leadership in these great tasks, in the tasks of building really an orchestra, in which everybody plays his instrument, but in which there is at least a common score.

We will have to tackle this task. Yet in our own immediate economic task we will have to do twice as well as we have done before. Here are all these "service employees," as Herman Kahn and Daniel Bell call them; that is, people who are not directly productive and who have to be supported by the directly productive ones. But they do want a high standard of living, and they do have to be well supported. Each employee and worker in the primary and secondary sector will have to support many more nonproducers. That means productivity of production workers will have to rise very fast, and this is management's first task.

Secondly, if we want to maintain our standard of living and our capacity for performance, we will have to tackle the productivity of the people who do not work with their hands—the knowledge workers, whether they are within the corporation, like market researchers, or whether they are in the schools or in government services. Their productivity is certainly not much above zero, and it certainly has not increased much. We have so far not improved the productivity of education any place. We have added numbers, and as we have added numbers of students we have proportionately increased the number of teachers, and nobody learns more than he did before. Many more people sit—whether anything happens to the rest of the anatomy we do not know. The productivity of education has not gone up, no matter how we measure it. The same thing is true of the hospitals and also of government. Knowledge-work has so far not shown any increasing productivity. Our predecessors around the turn of the century suddenly discovered that it is management's job to make the manual worker productive, and that productivity is not "working harder" but "working smarter." That job has yet to be tackled with respect to knowledge-work. So far we do not know how to do it for a very simple reason: we can count the number of shoes that go down a shoe production line, but how do we measure the output of an engineering department? Yet there are very few things less pleasing, either in heaven or on earth, than an engineering department that with great efficiency, great elegance, and great dispatch produces a drawing for the wrong product. How do you measure that? And if you cannot measure it, how do you work at productivity? The same is true in all knowledge-work.

We also need much more profitability. All the things the sociologists point out that society needs require a rapid increase in capital investment per worker, which can come only out of profit. The investment per knowledge-worker is much higher than that for even the most highly capitalized manual worker. A hospital bed requires more investment than any executive would dream of having in a plant for a worker. The same is true of investment in education and of any other knowledge-work. The average investment per manual worker in the United States is around $15,000–$25,000. The average investment per knowledge-worker is probably twice that, and it is going up. Where is this tremendous capital requirement going to come from? This is one of the main reasons for the worldwide capital shortage, which will therefore in all likelihood continue. This capital can come only out of profit. We will have to operate with greater and not with lower profitability and with far greater productivity. Add to this that it is not true that ours is a rich world. Ours is a poor world that suddenly has gotten the ambition of becoming affluent. Two-thirds of mankind are not richer than they were five hundred years ago. But they know that this is not ordained by God: by looking at Sweden or the United States they see that their condition can be changed. So they will have to be financed and above all their produc-

tivity will have to increase. If we have learned one thing
in the last one hundred years it is that distribution of
income does not create wealth. The only thing that creates wealth is to make the poor productive. This has been
the achievement of the developed nations. We will have
to do it on a worldwide scale, and that again means
higher productivity and higher profitability. So the economic task is not going to become less important. Herman Kahn pointed out that nobody will be thankful to us
if we do it. Yes, but if we do not do it, we will have quite
a few people who will be exceedingly critical of us, and
rightly so.

The economic implications of Bell's and Kahn's presentations are staggering. They mean not only that we
will have to do our traditional jobs better, we will have
to extend them into new areas where nobody yet knows
how to do the job. At the same time we will increasingly
be responsible for what the new catch phrase calls "the
quality of life," which is simply a new term for community. We will increasingly have to take responsibility for
our own social impacts, that is, for the things we do, not
because we have the slightest urge to do them, but because we cannot make shoes or build ships or manufacture tin cans or print textbooks without impacts outside
our own four walls. We will have to take responsibility
for them and look ahead and try to convert them into
opportunities. For the first job of a business manager is
to convert social needs into profitable opportunities.
The successful business manager does not make the
newspapers except on the financial page. He makes the
headlines, when he has failed in his job at anticipating
social needs and turning them into opportunities for

profitable business. Where we cannot convert our impacts into profitable business opportunity we will have to see what regulation is needed in the common interest, and we will have to anticipate what regulation is needed, whether we talk of the environment or of any other issue. We will have to take responsibility and anticipate what is needed by the way of social rules, precisely because we want to maintain and strengthen a free market, and we therefore must anticipate what rules and restraints are needed to enable us to function. What is needed today, so that five years from now we do not suddenly have a demand for a ban or a regulation which is unlikely to do the job? Government regulations rarely accomplish what they are intended to do, because they are always written in a crisis. There is an old lawyers' proverb that "sensational cases make very poor law" and scandals make very poor regulations. Unless we anticipate the needs whether for the protection of the resources of the ocean or of the physical environment and think through what the rules should be and then work at getting them, we will get the wrong rules. Do not blame the politicians. They will move in because we have failed in our job. Any complaint about antibusiness legislation is always really saying: We have not done our jobs when we had the time to do it. We waited, hoping the problem would go away —it never goes away. Then it becomes a scandal and then the politician must act. Do not blame him if he acts rashly and unwisely, because that is the only thing one can do in complex matters if one has to act fast.

We will also have to learn to take increasing leadership in developing management capacity outside of the business enterprise, both in the public-service institutions and in the developing countries. These are big jobs. If you were to ask me how does one do them, I would give you two answers. The first answer is the punch line of an old story about the consultant: "How dare you insult me, asking me how to do anything. I am a policy maker." You can probably write the beginning of the story yourself; I, too, am a policy maker. I never know how to do anything. I am a consultant, I get paid for putting other people to work and then criticizing them.

The second and more serious answer is that there is no one answer. If we try to find *one* answer we are going to end up with no answer. We need a great many different answers. We need diversity, we need different approaches, but most of all we need managers taking responsibility. A good many of my friends in business management resent these new demands and feel that they reflect antibusiness sentiment. They reflect something quite different, they reflect expectations that may be unrealistic. You and I know how limited managers are, how little they know and how busy they are, and that most are ordinary human beings. From the outside it does not look that way, we look far bigger, far stronger than we are, simply because of the performance record. These expectations are not "antibusiness." On the contrary, they reflect an overestimation of our capacity, of our wisdom, of our knowledge, and of our discipline.

But at the same time, let us be very careful that we do not fall into the opposite trap and glory in these new demands and new responsibilities, for we should not welcome them. My background was originally law, not economics. I learned many years ago that in constitutional law there is no responsibility without authority, and vice versa. Where one has no authority, one had better not take responsibility. Before taking on all those tasks which society today expects the businessman to take on, one should be very careful. It is sheer hubris, in the strictest Greek sense, to rush into responsibilities for which one has no authority. Rather than be happy and flattered by all these new demands, let us approach them in fear and trembling. They are demands to which we do not know the answer, demands which are not perhaps more difficult than anything the human race has ever tackled, but quite different and the different is usually much harder than the difficult. In order to do the new, one has to unlearn the old; while we are pretty good at learning we are horribly poor at unlearning. But let me also say that it does not help us to be unhappy about these demands. We will have to take them on. We will have to tackle them and we will have to do them well, simply because so much is at stake. Whether we want to or not, we have been chosen for that role. Those of you who served in a military service know that the dirtiest duty is the assignment one has "been volunteered for." The commanding officer says: I need volunteers, and you are one—those are the worst assignments. This is one of the assignments where we are "being volunteered" for by our boss: the society, and so we had better take it on.

In this pluralist society our critics, the young people —and one listens to the critics—want to destroy the institutions. They see a reality: the world has suddenly become an institutionalized world and what they are being told in their schools by their teachers about the structure of the world, which is essentially what was written in the seventeenth century, simply no longer makes sense. Neither sociology nor economics nor political science describes the world they live in and know. Their first reaction, and it is an understandable one, is to get rid of these institutions. The machine wreckers 170 years ago also thought that the way to handle a new reality was to get rid of it. It is not perhaps without irony to realize that within fifteen years after the worst Luddite riot in England the steam locomotive appeared and with it the triumph of the machine. I have a suspicion that we are very much in the same position. The institutions are not going to be destroyed. So far the only effect of the rebellion of the young has been to make administration far stronger than it has ever been. In the university the young are destroying the faculties—that may be a very wholesome and healthy thing to do, but that is not their intention. They are making administration far stronger, they are not making it weaker. They are not going to destroy the institutions, simply because they are not willing nor is the modern world able to do without the services these institutions perform. Nothing amuses me quite as much as listening to those wonderful ballads of the young about returning to nature, sung on an electric guitar in front of a microphone. The young are not going to destroy these institutions, but they are at least highlighting and identifying the task. Our task is to make the institutions perform, not only their own specific task which some of them do quite well and others do quite poorly, but in addition to that the task of building a community. While every single institution and its leadership face this demand, the one who is expected to take the lead, to show the way, and to take responsibility for better and worse, is business leadership. And this is a new role, this is a new reality, and this, I submit, is what we are going to be expected to perform not only in the 1980s but right now.

DONALD C. BURNHAM, born in 1915, graduated from Purdue University in 1936 with a bachelor of science degree in mechanical engineering. He spent the early part of his career with General Motors Corporation, becoming Assistant Chief Engineer of the Oldsmobile Division, before joining Westinghouse in 1954 as Vice-President in Charge of Manufacturing. He was chosen in 1962 to head the group of divisions that develops, builds, and sells systems to improve industrial production. He was elected President in 1963 and became Chairman in 1969.

D. C. Burnham is the recipient of an honorary doctorate of engineering from Purdue University and also of honorary degrees from Drexel Institute of Technology, Polytechnic Institute of Brooklyn, and Indiana Institute of Technology. He is a member of the Business Council, the International Advisory Council of Chase Manhattan Bank of New York, and a life trustee of the Carnegie-Mellon University.

Corporate Planning and Social Problems
DONALD C. BURNHAM

One of America's great men—Theodore Roosevelt—once said "nine-tenths of wisdom consists in being wise in time." So it is in laying long-range plans. There is no better time than now, at the turn of a decade, for doing this. Whenever we enter a new decade, even those people who consider tomorrow "long range" stop to look farther ahead. Because they are in a new decade, they may even talk wistfully about "ten years from now."

But how few people, even some hard-headed businessmen, actually plan that far ahead. And we are so used to hearing references to the "1980s," in terms of far-out speculation and wishful thinking, that we resist bringing that swiftly approaching time into any clear focus.

There are four key considerations which I believe must go into our long-range planning if we are to arrive at the 1980s in better business condition than we are today—four fundamentals which, if slighted, will guarantee failure of almost any business enterprise during the decade ahead.

The first of these brings me immediately into conflict with those people in America—and I presume in other countries—who say that no longer should we seek more and more—who say that we should instead be satisfied with less, presumably to protect the quality of life which now is being threatened by the size of the problems facing us.

But people will continue to demand more and better satisfaction of their needs, whether the needs by for products to make life easier or more rewarding, or for services to make it more enjoyable or convenient. And the business that survives and flourishes into the 1980s will be the one that has become more productive, thus meeting these needs in larger measure.

So the first fundamental to be considered in long-range planning is the need to plan for *continual improvement in productivity.* I strongly disagree with those who say our efforts to improve the quality of life are threatened by a productive industry.

People in the service industries—such as government, education, health care, and similar professions which now employ twice as many people in the United States as does manufacturing industry—all of these people want an improved standard of living and they are demanding and getting higher pay. However, their productivity has not improved very much—certainly not enough to justify the improvement in living standards which they want and which their dedication and effort deserves.

We must learn how to improve their productivity. And I believe it can be done by applying some of the same principles which industry has applied in the factory; things like better equipment, new management methods, better training. Once these techniques have been successfully applied, then the efforts of the service industries to gain higher wages will not just result in inflation but will really give these people a higher living standard because they will be producing more. This point is too often forgotten when it comes to the question of improving the quality of life.

The solution of many of the world's ills—pollution for example—is going to require a lot of time, money, and effort. We can get them only by improving our productivity in the other things we do—generating the means to tackle these social and cultural problems and programs without sacrificing our material gains. Productivity improvement provides the basis for social and cultural progress at the same time it is bringing more products to the marketplace.

So no matter what we desire—be it more things, better quality of life, cultural advancement—we must indeed improve our productivity in the 1970s so we can afford the money, time, and effort these things require. Productivity improvement is not only compatible with a better quality of life, it is essential to it.

How do we go about getting this improvement? By planning for it. Whether it is a service or a manufacturing activity—no matter what it is—productivity is improved by doing a better job of planning. It doesn't improve itself. And we must organize for the job.

The department which can improve its productivity five per cent this year is the one which is likely to improve its productivity five per cent again next year. The department that makes only one per cent improvement this year probably will only make one per cent again next year.

The difference is that the first department has people spending time planning for this improvement—doing research in new methods and new materials, developing new procedures—so that its products and services can be supplied more effectively.

A business has to plan for new facilities which will produce improved products at lower cost; it must plan new procedures which will cut down on paperwork and reduce overhead expenses; it must plan to develop its managers and engineers, training them in the ways to improve their performance.

The office secretary may ask, "How in the world can *my* job be made more efficient and productive?" In reply, I would point out to her that some of the most rapidly growing and successful businesses in the world today are the ones which are helping people like her improve their productivity. We have seen a recent revolution in office machines which are helping the long-neglected office force do its job faster and better.

On top of all these things must be provided the incentive and enthusiasm to continue productivity improvement efforts. This can be done by giving productivity improvement top priority in the planning procedure. A wise man has said it is pleasant to think that you have done a good job—but it is fatal to think that you have done a perfect job. The business that gives high priority in its planning to productivity improvement will never make that fatal assumption.

The second fundamental consideration in long-range planning is the recognition that the strength of a business and industry rests on *excellence*. Excellence, I would suggest, must permeate every aspect of our operations. There must be excellence of management—capable people, well motivated, carefully placed in jobs they can do best. Excellence of product—high-quality materials and components, good design, top craftsmanship, stringent quality control. Excellence of service—prompt deliveries, careful handling, determination to please each customer, a willingness to rectify errors quickly and courteously.

Anyone who doubts the importance of excellence should study a list of companies who have gone out of business. Some were the buggy-whip manufacturers who failed to seek new markets in changing times. But many more were companies that drifted into a fool's paradise where economy or expediency was mistaken as an adequate substitute for quality.

One of the most remarkable aspects of excellence is that it is highly contagious. Not long ago, a major American trade magazine announced its annual selection of the ten most outstanding manufacturing plants completed in my country last year. I hope you won't consider it immodest if I mention that two of my company's plants were on that list. The previous year we also had one, and one the year before that. These awards were particularly gratifying to me because the basis for judging them is overall excellence—in planning and construction. More than 150 engineering specifications and construction details were considered by the judges. They considered the appearance of the plant, its pollution-control devices, its electrical services, its medical facilities, its ventilating system, and so on.

I mention this because I think success in these areas reflects many different departments endeavoring to outdo each other in striving for excellence. When excellence is the hallmark of the various parts of a company, excellence is the hallmark of the company as a whole.

It takes a long time to bring excellence to maturity. For that reason, attention to the principle of excellence should be a major ingredient of industry's long-range planning.

A third fundamental consideration in long-range planning is the recognition that the decade ahead will be a *consumer-oriented* one. And so will be the decades beyond.

Already the consumer has found a voice and made himself heard in many fields. Automobile manufacturers have had to respond to these voices with a variety of new safety devices. The auto makers and oil companies have stepped up their research and development efforts to find a satisfactory improvement or replacement for today's internal combustion engines and high-performance gasolines. Industries such as steel and paper are being forced to spend vast sums to curb water and air pollution. The electric-power industry is being pressed to find ways to avoid the effects of warm water discharged from generating stations. Appliance manufacturers are facing stringent new safety restrictions. Advertising and product warranties are being subjected to careful scrutiny by an increasingly demanding public.

The message from all this is clear. A key to success in the decades ahead will be reliability and high quality in product and service. We have to recognize that the needs of people are going to receive major attention in the years ahead. These needs will include the health, comfort, and convenience of people. Not just wealthy people—all people. It will concern their homes, their offices, their factories, their schools.

The businessman who can meet people's needs will find that there is a continuing, growing market for his products and services. The time to consider what these future needs will be is now. Only by planning now can we be sure of having the capabilities to meet those needs of the future.

The fourth and last key consideration for long-range planning may have a familiar ring in view of recent events. It is the need to *become involved* in the society around us—the end of business isolationism. All the evidence that I have seen points to the fact that, in the years ahead of us, there will be no place for the business isolationist—the individual who simply manages his own business and attempts to remain aloof from the problems that are plaguing the society around him.

He will have to recognize that these problems of society are problems that affect him, his customers, and his employes. And so inevitably they will affect his business and will determine whether the business is to succeed or fail.

We have to get involved with our governments, our universities and schools—involved in our environmental problems and with our young people. I don't mean to suggest that we should go out and govern our cities or run our universities. But we do have to get involved to the point where we understand what the real problems of our society are. Then we have to decide what we can contribute to their solution, and how we can make that contribution, and then do it.

As businessmen, we pride ourselves on our ability to

get jobs done—to get problems solved—in the least expensive and the most efficient way. With an increasing number of technological problems besetting our cities and our nations, we are being challenged, particularly by our young people, to demonstrate that we can help solve society's problems. Eliminating environmental pollution is one example.

In America, the one sure way to attract a capacity audience on a college campus is to get a businessman to speak on the environment. But such a speaker should keep in mind a comment by Winston S. Churchill when he once was congratulated on his ability to draw large audiences. "It is quite flattering," he said, "but I always remember that if, instead of making a speech I was going to be hanged, the crowd would be twice as big." Our college audiences, one feels, come not so much for the businessman's speech as for his hanging.

Perhaps it is because of this defensive posture that many of us may feel awkward in addressing ourselves to social problems that traditionally have been left to governmental agencies and public institutions. And we feel even more uneasy when we encounter delays, overlapping authority for decisions, time-consuming legal requirements, and undesirable political considerations instead of the well-ordered procedures of the world of private business. These we will have to learn how to live with and deal with.

But these problems around us are not just obligations to be faced. They also are markets for our products and services. They are timely opportunities for us to serve, for the benefit of the public and for the benefit of our stockholders.

Just consider the transportation problems that confront commuters in almost every major city in the world. Consider these problems in terms of business opportunities for the manufacturers of transit cars, buses, control and communications equipment, propulsion systems. Think of the business potential these problems offer makers of steel, aluminum, glass, and the hundreds of other components that are needed in a modern transportation system.

The transportation people in my own company look admiringly at what has been done in Stockholm. We know that eventually other cities will recognize the abundant blessings of a modern transit system and want the same for themselves. Our plans have been laid to be ready to serve that demand when it develops. It has been said that when plans are laid in advance, it is surprising how often circumstances fit in with them. We are impatiently waiting and preparing for that to happen in rapid transit.

It is time to think of the future and present problems of the corporation, not as problems, but as potential opportunities for business. And these are opportunities whose solution will not just benefit the corporate structure, but society as a whole.

HISAMICHI KANO, born in Tokyo in 1911, received his education in the United States, England, and Japan. He graduated from Kyoto Imperial University in 1938. In 1946 he formed Mercury Services Inc., a public relations company, in Tokyo. In 1954 he joined Ray-O-Vac Company (Japan) Ltd. after having assisted in its formation. Ray-O-Vac Company (Japan) is a joint venture of Tokyo Shibaura Electric Co., Ltd. and ESB Incorporated of Philadelphia. The same year he became Director of the New Asia Trade News Agency, Ltd., into which Mercury Services Inc. was merged. In 1956 he became Director of the Asia Advertising Agency Inc.

Hisamichi Kano is one of the leading advisers to foreign businesses in Japan.

Managing for the Future
in Japanese Industry
HISAMICHI KANO

As Westerners are doubtless aware, the Japanese economy has been growing rather rapidly. It is as shocking and frightening to us as it is astounding and bewildering to others. Yet, because we are caught in this tremendous upsurge, we have become accustomed in the past fifteen years or so to see progress, not as a steady onward advance, but as acceleration, as increase of the rate of growth. This, undoubtedly, is an unmistakable sign of immaturity. But the forces impelling progressive growth are there. They cannot be choked off or stilled. They have, however, been fairly well harnessed to provide the drive for our own development. Because Japan is growing our yardstick is applied not to the growth itself, but to the increment of the rate of growth. So it goes with our planning: growth is normal, and advancement calls for faster than normal growth.

A phenomenon such as this undoubtedly has many complex roots. My own life spans more than half a century of modern Japan. Yet I am no more able than anyone else to give you a clear and concise explanation. We Japanese are as puzzled as any Westerner. But for many years, I have had to try to explain to many Western friends how we do things; and out of these efforts have come some idea of what the causes may have been. There are some basic characteristics which, although they may not be the answer, appear to me to be highly important factors which are not fully understood in the West, or for that matter even in Japan. Outstanding among these factors are:

1. Our national and individual commitment to "catching up."
2. The use of organization as a team, with authority coming down from the top and ideas extending upward from the bottom for joint decision making.
3. The extensive and general use of "planning" as a means to weld together national and business goals, and also business and individual goals. Let me say a few words about each of these.

For nearly a century, ever since Japan was opened to the West, our grandparents and parents regarded as their central duty and task the building of a modern industrialized state. They had the slogan "wealthy nation–strong soldiers" and their model was the great powers of Europe at that time. To this end, it was early realized that the highest priority would have to be given to foreign trade, so there was, until our military establishment was crushed and dismantled in 1945, a constant struggle going on between the trade-oriented business leaders and the militarists who opted for territorial expansion. But the real objective in either case was to catch up with the West. How this catching up was actually achieved is something which eludes explantion. Quite frankly, I would not be able to tell you what it was that brought about this transformation from a basically agrarian economy to a modern industrialized nation in the short space of just one century. I have lived through more than half this period, and have seen, and am seeing, astounding changes that appear to be transmutations.

Yet, beneath the surface, I do not think the change is at all as big as it appears. We are still compulsively striving to be bigger and better than the other fellow. My own parents often admonished me when I was a small child to "do double the work of anybody else." We in business, in government, in education, have been deeply engrossed in our daily tasks, blindly believing that by doing just a little more we would be doing our own bit to "catch up with the West." We have not had the time nor have we directed conscious effort, to think about what to do once our century-old dream of working and living and playing "as they do in the West" became a reality.

This ingrained urge to excel, together with the setting of a common goal, could explain in large measure the unique organization of Japanese society in which forces that are separate and often in conflict—government and business, for instance, and business and teachers—are closely linked in a network of relationships—some formal, most informal—which create a national consensus on what "catching up" means or should mean. Perhaps the Western critics who speak of "Japan Incorporated," and see the whole nation as one giant business organization bent on competing with the West overemphasize one aspect of modern Japan. But it is a true aspect, to which we too half jokingly refer as "Hinomaru Kaisha"—the Rising Sun Company. The essence of the Japanese effort of the past hundred years is that this goal of catching up with and surpassing the West at its own game became the aim of every Japanese business (and also nonbusiness, such as our universities and hospitals) and government agency and of everyone from management down to the lowliest worker in our organizations.

You have doubtless heard a good deal of how Japanese businesses work as a team, as an "extended family." Perhaps a few words of illustration will tell you more than volumes of sociological analyses. In our office work we in Japan operate, I would say, in a most unique way. For instance, the Japanese executive's secretary is a receptionist, phone-tender, filing clerk, refreshments-server, errand-runner, and perhaps an eye-soother, but virtually never a note-taker. The reason for this, of course, is our enslavement by the Chinese ideograms and their derivative Japanese phonetic symbols that we use in our writing. Most of our business communications are handwritten. To have one typed out is almost impossible because the Japanese typewriter—the typewriter capable of writing Chinese ideograms and Japanese phonetics—is a huge machine almost as big as an upright piano. It carries about two thousand characters on the standard tray and an additional two thousand underneath in auxiliary trays which have to be picked out by forceps when a character is missing. In using this typewriter the only advantage over script is that you can do about fifteen copies at a time, and that is the only labor-saving use it serves. Therefore, most of our office writing is done by hand.

Top managers almost never write or draft official business letters. The only scribblings they are addicted to are scrawls on small slips of paper as confidential notes to associates or subordinates, or on the margins of correspondence and other papers indicating what action is required of whom. This absence of stenographers and formal interoffice letters reduces to the absolute minimum individual direction and management on a person-to-person basis: and important matters are always studied and discussed by the management team.

The third characteristic, the welding together of our goals and society, is the result of a continuing process which we call "planning." Outwardly, this function has many resemblances to what you in the West mean by the term "planning." But in Japan, because of the teamwork involved in any organization, even the smallest businesses operate on the basis of plans which call for weeks and maybe months of study and discussion at all levels of management. The process of plan formulation actually creates, through active participation, a concrete and detailed image of what is to be expected. Also, this process to us is a way of meshing individual effort and performance with company (and also national) objectives. It is as much a social as it is an economic or business process.

A very general picture of what can be expected to transpire is provided at the government level. On April 9, 1970, the Economic Council, working for Prime Minister Sato, submitted its five-year plan for social and economic development on which it had been working since January 1969. This new plan which, for want of a better name is called the New Socio-Economic Development Plan, supersedes the Socio-Economic Development Plan which was officially adopted in March 1967 to cover the five-year period ending March 1972. The key objectives of this New Plan are:

1. Realization of an economy and society which is rich in humanity.
2. A real annual economic growth rate of 10.6 per cent on the average for the coming years.
3. Average annual rise of consumer prices to be not more than 4.4 per cent, with not more than 3.8 per cent gain in the final year of the plan. (This is very optimistic.)
4. Average annual growth rate of personal income to be at 12.1 per cent.
5. Per capita national income in the 1975–76 fiscal year to be $2,750 (2.5 times the amount in 1968–69).
6. Achievement of higher efficiency in agriculture and other activities, as measured by international standards.
7. Average annual growth rate of public investment at 13.5 per cent, as against the 10.7 per cent of the old plan, with efforts directed toward prevention of public hazards and traffic accidents.

Not one of the previous plans was satisfactory as a working pattern because the estimates of growth were overconservative. For instance, the plan adopted in 1967 set the growth rate target at 8.2 per cent, whereas in reality the rates in 1967 and 1968 were well over 10 per cent. So this time, econometric simulations were performed, using seven different models, to compute the most plausible rates. Incidentally, one of the basic assumptions was that the average annual growth rate of world trade would be 7.5 per cent, which is somewhat lower than what is foreseen by the economists in the United Nations and the OECD.

This may sound very modern and "twentieth century"—and so it is. But our great-grandparents, including my own grandfather who at eighteen was among the last *daimyo** serving the Tokugawa Shogunate, followed very similar processes—without computers and without elaborate statistics—in regard to their projects such as the adoption almost overnight of the Western calendar and method of timekeeping, complete overhaul of the judiciary and penal systems, the attainment of universal literacy in twenty or thirty years, and thousands of other programs for remaking Japan into a "modern" nation. What we are doing today is refining the method which has been working for Japan for a whole century.

Today, for instance, there is a private nonprofit organization supported by the electric-power industry, which concerns itself with rather large-scale planning for the future. Heading this Council for Industrial Planning is Yasuzaemon Matsunaga, revered as "the grand old man of electric power," who also presides over the Central Research Institute of the Electric Power Industry, which, besides research and experimentation in power generation, transmission, and distribution, conducts studies on the energy needs and resources of Japan.

My late father, who died seven years ago, was active in the Industrial Planning group, and in the late fifties was already advocating, with carefully prepared facts and

*One of the feudal lords.

figures, the reclamation of 800 square kilometers of Tokyo Bay to provide an ideal site for the expansion needs of Tokyo. He also proposed that the Imperial Palace, the former Edo Castle, be vacated because the city center, with growing air pollution and traffic noise, was "no fitting place for the Emperor and his family to live." The Council also pioneered in input-output analysis, using the island of Hokkaido as an exercise case; and it urged the building of a high dam at the upper reaches of the Tone River to ensure adequate future supply of industrial and drinking water for Tokyo and its environs.

Mention has already been made of the Economic Council, which assists the Government in formulating what might be called a "master plan" for the nation's development. The big industrial groups, such as the Mitsubishi, Sumitomo, and Mitsui Groups, as well as the newer and smaller industry clusters around Toyota, Fujikura, C. Itoh, and others, are establishing their own "think tanks" for large-scale planning and coordinated activity in such growth areas as multinational ventures, overseas manufacturing and distribution, ocean development, urban renewal, environmental engineering, and space exploration. Thus "planning" is not left to the government, although any successful project eventually is reflected in government plans and policies.

For communication between business and government at the national level there are, in addition to the opportunities offered by the many media of information, established channels provided by the organizations representing business, banking, and industry. The Federation of Economic Organizations (Keidanren), the Japan Committee for Economic Development (Keizai

Doyukai), and the Japan Chamber of Commerce and Industry (Nissho) present and discuss with top-level government personnel and politicians the views held by businessmen on industrial structure, economic plans, population, monetary measures, foreign trade and exchange, pollution, farm policy, and other matters of national importance.

Perhaps the best way to illustrate how all this works would be to take a not so very hypothetical example—a small company, small not only by Japanese but by any standard—and see how it forms its own plans on the basis of the government plan, and how it uses planning to obtain direction and dedication through acceptance of objectives throughout its organization. Our company is the Medetai Medallion Kabushiki Kaisha. Our capital is 50 million yen, our assets about 700 million yen, and our annual sales are about 1,150 million yen.* We have about 370 employees.

Let us assume that our day-to-day business is running smoothly according to the guidelines provided by our weekly, monthly, and quarterly schedules for sales, production, personnel, and facilities improvements and expansion, as well as by our annual budget. How do we go about planning for the years to come? From the government prediction, we know that our economy is expected to grow on the average at an annual rate of about 14 per cent, not allowing for price rises. This means that, in our case, we must plan for at least the same rate of expansion if we want to maintain our relative standing. We next turn to what our own industry expects. Most of

*360 yen = one U.S. dollar (1970).—Ed.

the businesses in Japan have their own local and national organizations which provide fairly trustworthy figures on production, shipments, and market shares, both domestic and export. With the data from our association, we are therefore able to ascertain our own position in our industry, and to set targets for our growth plan in the hope that we shall be doing better, and grow faster, than any of our competitors.

If we were a subsidiary or a close affiliate of any of the really big companies, we would probably be provided with another set of figures from the parent company's long-range plan which usually includes subsidiary operations. Now, with all the outside and inside information it can gather and digest, our planning section of the general-affairs department plunges into the task of revising and adding to our current five-year plan. For this, it must of course consult every department within our organization, to make close guesses as to what can be expected in sales, production, work-force availability, wage increases, materials prices, and other factors bearing upon our future performance. These consultations and meetings are countless and seemingly endless, with many a heated argument. But finally, mainly because the deadline set by top management is fast approaching, the plan begins to emerge in its final form. At this stage a meeting of the department heads, with top management present, is held for explanation of all the details and for last-minute changes.

The next step is formal adoption of the plan. By this time, of course, all department heads as well as top management are quite familiar with the proposal. But there must be formal approval before the plan can be propagated within our company organization. This is where our *ringi* system comes into play. The Chinese characters for the word *ringi* denote "presentation for discussion." But the currently accepted connotation is "request for permission." Our planning section, in charge of the long-range plan, writes the *ringisho*, (request for permission document) to which the seals of the person drafting the proposal (in our case the head of section) and of the head of the general affairs department are stamped. The paper, with the draft plan attached, is then circulated among all the department heads involved, each of whom affixes his seal to signify concurrence. Upon completion of this round, the papers pass upward to the top management group for their seals of approval. This is the procedure that is followed in most Japanese companies and also in most Japanese government and public institutions.

So much for today and the recent past. After a hundred years of concentrated effort we have come to the level to which we had long aspired. We can now hold our own with the most advanced nations of the West, not by military might but in peaceful competition in education, in technology, and in the economy. What about the future?

Like anyone else we are anxious to know what the future holds for us, to be able to make decisions for the coming years without too much fear of going wrong, particularly in regard to large capital appropriations and spending. As I have said before, we have tended to be too preoccupied with keeping up with the surging growth of the economy. But is this the right way to proceed? Do we have a correct grasp of the situation in a nonisolated world? This creeping doubt has given rise to an uneasiness and to a feeling that perhaps a pause, a respite, a slowing down of the headlong rush is now in order, for more thought to be given to the present and the future.

This I personally welcome. For without doubts as to where we are headed, without doubts as to one's personal convictions, can there be any real comprehension of the challenges we must face? We have strained to build up the productive facilities needed to sustain a decent standard of living, and this has been achieved, thanks to Providence and to the drive generated by the feeling of thankfulness for having been spared. So today, there is growing a reflective mood, with the realization that there is more to life than sheer struggle for survival, that we must share in the joys and sorrows of the world, and that as generators of wealth we must aspire to a better and more livable environment for ourselves and the people who are gainfully participating in our operations.

HERMAN KAHN, born in 1922, holds a B.A. degree in physics and mathematics from the University of California (1945), and an M.S. degree in physics from California Institute of Technology (1948). He was associated with The RAND Corporation, where he worked on problems in applied physics and mathematics, operations research and systems analysis, civil defense and strategic warfare.

In 1961 he left RAND to help found Hudson Institute. Among his major interests as director of Hudson Institute are studies on Latin American and other development problems, inquiries into alternative world futures and long run (10–35 years) political, economic, technological, and cultural changes. He has served as a consultant to many government committees as well as to numerous industrial and scientific concerns.

Among his books are *On Thermonuclear War* (1960); *Thinking About the Unthinkable* (1962); *On Escalation* (1965); with Anthony J. Wiener, *The Year 2000* (1967); *The Emerging Japanese Superstate* (1970); and, with B. Bruce-Briggs, *Things to Come* (1972).

Forces for Change
HERMAN KAHN

Despite its great publicity as one of the forces of corporate change, I think the "information-explosion" as it is commonly discussed is greatly exaggerated as a problem. Some caveats are necessary relating to issues associated with the "aging" expert, technological revolutions, and doctrinal lags, and I will take account of some of these in a moment. But I don't know of any normal professional area today, with the possible exception of computer technology, where the top researchers, at least, are not familiar with all of the important work being done in their professions.

However, there are two important and related information-explosion type problems. The first is the problem of a professional or a generalist who wishes to learn his neighbor's area without spending a great deal of time on it. The second is the problem of the expert who finds most of his information increasingly obsolete—i.e., that he is becoming less of an expert—and who nonetheless does not wish to take the time to study the necessary papers and reports even though they are readily available. Learning your neighbor's field or keeping current in your own are often very difficult jobs today, but these

97

are less problems of information retrieval as of the formulation and exposition of relatively available information in such a way as to facilitate learning and then to encourage the learning. In particular, one can focus on the task of formulating and expositing of information so as to be able, rapidly and accurately, to transfer this information to serious, highly motivated and well-informed people, and, second, to do this in a manner that makes it possible for them to delve further on their own. I will refer to these respectively as the "propaedeutic" and "heuristic" issues; they are related to the "information-explosion" concept but are quite different in both denotation and connotation.

There are a number of these non-issues and I might as well list and dismiss the most obvious. For example I will not refer to unemployment in the developed nations due to the elimination of unskilled jobs as a byproduct of the advance of modern technology and automation. Despite continuing "propaganda," this has been shown by a number of studies to be largely a non-issue, or at least a misleading description of the phenomenon being described. Rather paradoxically, this sometimes is' an issue in underdeveloped nations—particularly if minimum wage levels have been set at unrealistically high levels, thus making it uneconomic even for low-grade or marginal industries to employ unskilled labor.

Another non-issue in its usual formulation is the worldwide maldistribution of income. This is usually formulated as an issue of eliminating "gaps"—of decreasing the separation between the richest and the poorest.

There are a very large number of such non-issues which often are included in discussions of the future. Hopefully, most of them are not included here.

What we are trying to do in the Hudson Institute study of the future is first and foremost to create a framework in which it is possible to have a serious discussion among a rather large community of participants. This particular project is much bigger than our usual kind of study—in part because it is being done in cooperation with nearly one hundred major corporations around the world. These corporations are not only helping to finance the effort but also participate actively in formulating and conducting the research and exposition. Also involved are several cooperating research organizations, many consultants, and of course, the thirty-five to forty permanent staff members of the Hudson Institute.

One of the biggest problems we find in this project is the lack of a shared literature able to provide a source of commonly understood metaphors, analogies, concepts, examples, and even vocabulary and jargon. I believe that one of the main reasons the American Constitutional Convention of 1787 did such a magnificent job was that the delegation possessed—in clear contrast with us—an extraordinarily rich shared background of experience, understanding, typologies, concepts, and theories. Almost all of them had been men of affairs. They all knew the Bible, the classics, and Shakespeare. Most of them had probably read Gibbon, Adam Smith, and the French encyclopedists. There is no such shared general culture today among professionals, officials, and executives in the West, or even in any particular country. You cannot find in any ordinary discussion or study group this kind of rich common source of allusion, metaphor, reference, example, and analysis.

We recently held a conference on the Hudson study in Paris. Most of the participants were from European and North American corporations, with some from Latin America and Japan. I seriously suggested, with the kind of hubris common to many staff members of the Hudson Institute, our "Synoptic Context," a ten-page booklet of summary charts, or some revised version of it, would eventually become—at least for the Hudson study on Policy Issues of the seventies and the eighties—a reasonable substitute for the Bible, the Koran, Shakespeare, Adam Smith, Goethe, Heine, Montesquieu, Comte, and Voltaire. There was a stunned silence, as the audience absorbed the fact that I really meant it. They thought for a few more minutes and then one man got up in indignation and said, "Why have you omitted Dante?" Whether or not the "Synoptic Context," even revised and/or elaborated, can really be used in such a way is, of course, highly problematical. Nevertheless, we are trying to produce such a document—or at least formulate and exposite such a framework.

Let me now turn to what we call the "surprise-free projection." It lists, roughly in order of estimated significance and importance, seventeen broad (and overlapping) issues and trends which are likely to concern us in the next decade or two and which I would judge to be the main forces making for change during the next two decades.

RELATIVELY A-MILITARY, RELATIVELY A-POLITICAL, "SURPRISE-FREE PROJECTIONS" OF THE "MOST SIGNIFICANT" ASPECTS OF THE FINAL THIRD OF THE TWENTIETH CENTURY

A. Continuation and/or topping out of multifold trend.

B. Onset of postindustrial culture in nations with 20–30 per cent of the world's population and in enclaves elsewhere.

C. "Political settlement" of World War II—including the rise of Japan to being the third superpower and the reemergence of both Germanies.

D. The coming 1985 technological crisis—need for worldwide (but probably ad hoc) "zoning ordinances" and other controls.

E. With important exceptions, an erosion of the twelve traditional societal levers, a corresponding search for meaning and purpose and the creation of some cultural confusion.

F. Onset and impact of various new political milieus, e.g., rise of a "Humanist Left"–"Responsible Center" confrontation—in the high (visible) culture of the West.

G. Increasingly "revisionist" Communism, capitalism, and Christianity in Europe and Western hemisphere.

H. A general decrease in consensus and authority—a general increased diversity (and some increased polarization) in ideology, in value systems, and in life styles.

I. Worldwide (foreign and domestic) "Law and Order" issues.

J. Populist and/or "conservative" backlash and revolts.

K. Increasing problem (worldwide) of trained incapacity and/or illusioned or irrelevant argumentation.

L. Better understanding and techniques for sustained economic development for rich and poor—high (2–15 per cent) annual growth in GNP/CAP almost everywhere—the green revolution and a worldwide capability for modern industry and technology—growing importance of multinational corporations and conglomerates.

M. Nativist, messianic, or other "irrationally" emotional mass and elitist movements—decrease in rational politics.

N. Many chronic crises—(e.g., four divided countries, Arab-Israeli conflict, Sino-Soviet, and Sino-U.S. hostility, etc.)

O. Much new conflict and turmoil in Afro-Asia and perhaps Latin America and non-Communist Far East.

P. A relative multipolar and anarchic but also relatively orderly and unified world—i.e., enormous growth in world trade, communications, and travel; limited development of international and multinational institutions; some relative decline in the power, influence and, prestige of U.S. and U.S.S.R.; new "intermediate powers" emerge: e.g., East Germany, Brazil, Mexico, Indonesia, Egypt, Argentina, etc.; a possible challenge by Japan for world leadership of some sort, China and Europe both rise and fall.

Q. Some "nonsignificant" surprises and perhaps some significant ones also.

The title includes the term "Surprise-Free Projections." Such a projection is not the same as the "naive projection" in economics, where one fixes some of the parameters and lets others change naturally. "Surprise-free" is a slightly more sophisticated concept. One puts into the projection any theory one believes. If the projection works out according to this theory one surely should not be surprised. It was your own theory—hence the term "surprise-free." You can have several and even contradictory surprise-free projections, since it is perfectly possible to hold, at least tentatively, several different theories that need not be consistent. It would not be surprising, in other words, if any one of them comes out. Generally "surprise-free projections" are relatively plausible projections, even if they are not predictions. However, they need not have this characteristic[1] of being plausible—at least they need not seem plausible without any argumentation.

There are, of course, a number of ways of looking ahead or of "creating anticipations," among them:

1. Imaginative and/or contingent scenarios.

2. Various projections (including "naive" and "surprise-free").

3. Forecasts.

4. Predictions.

5. Prophecies and revelations.

The first, as the title indicates, can be thought of as a special kind of science fiction or fantasy-type of scenario written to elaborate, perhaps in some detail, some theme or some contingent possibility. The second thing we can do is to record and interpret our past experience and then project this interpretation into the future, with various kinds of rules and more or less-sophisticated techniques, including the possible use of the "naive" and/or "surprise-free" projections I have been discussing. Almost by definition, such a projection makes no claim to be a statement about the future, but simply claims to be what it is—a projection of one interpretation of the past into the future which may or may not have any connotation or denotation of prediction about it. However, it is valuable to be able to demonstrate plausibility.

As far as actually foretelling the future is concerned, one can distinguish between forecast, prediction, and prophecy. The forecast, in effect, describes the various horses running in the race—i.e., the various types of events which could occur. It also tries to give some feeling or information about the relative probabilities of the various possibilities sometimes quantitatively, usually more or less qualitatively, and with more or less credibility. In the case of a prediction, one possibility is singled out as being almost overwhelmingly likely, and therefore the argument is made that this is what is probably going to happen. Prophecies and revelations are also predictions, but they usually rest on nonlogical or suprarational sources of authority and have a kind of moral or religious fervor behind them.

In discussing "surprise-free projections" I usually add that if the prediction is for a long period of time and over a large area of possibilities—as is true for our basic "surprise–free projection"—the most surprising thing that could occur is no surprises. Hence there is a kind of paradox in the concept. Actually, as I indicate, there are two kinds of surprises which could occur: "significant surprises" which would change the projection and "not significant surprises" which, important and dramatic as they might be, do not change the items on the chart to any great degree.

It is common at Hudson to emphasize the likelihood of significant surprises and therefore also to emphasize that this basic surprise-free chart is a projection and not a prediction. By doing so, one seems reasonably modest and careful, even scholarly. Yet you do not detract much from most peoples interest in the list if you emphasize that it is just a context set forth for the purpose of discussion and as much to be disagreed with as to be used as is. Nevertheless I would like to take a different position today. I have been looking at versions of this list for about five years, have been studying all the issues on it, and have come increasingly to believe that it is a rather likely prediction for the next decade or two—that for many purposes it can—and should—be made a major basis for planning. But whether you take my position or the more skeptic one of the majority of the Hudson staff should make little difference to our discussion today; it still makes sense to go over each item of the projection, even if in some cases only very lightly. I believe the chart does present a most plausible and useful context for discussion—whether or not it is to be taken as seriously as I suggest.

From the military and political points of view, the "surprise-free projections" in this list, whether we take them seriously as predictions or just as a useful analytic context, do not make up a very startling set of possibilities, particularly if we compare them with what actually happened in the first and second thirds of this century. That is why the terms "a-political" and "a-military" appear in the title. With the important exception of the rise of Japan, nothing on this chart suggests anything politically or militarily so dramatic as World War I, the destruction of the East European empires, the rise of Communism, the Great Depression, the effect of all of these in changing Western values and morale, the rise of fascism, World War II, the fall of fascism and the second rise of Communism, the decline of Europe, the Cold War, the decolonialization of the Third World, the detente, the Sino-Soviet split, and so on.

Thus I imply—even in noting the persistence of many current chronic political troubles—that today's map of the world, or at least today's political maps of North and South America, of most of Western Europe, of most of Eastern Europe and of the Soviet Union, China, and Japan, will probably still be largely valid for the year 2000. No doubt there may be frontier changes in parts of Afro-Asia, but in most of the world I would be surprised if today's maps were not reasonably accurate thirty years from today. This was not true for the earlier part of this century; there is a very big difference between this projection for the last quarter of the twentieth century and what actually happened during the first three-quarters of the century. In a longer discussion we could consider a number of examples of how military or political events could dramatically affect the final third of our century, but none of these seem very plausible, though no doubt some of them, or things like them, will occur, which is to say that *there will be surprises.*

An analogy that I like to use is that of the period

between 1815 and 1914. We know from the speeches, diaries, and letters of the people concerned, had the diplomats who were at the Congress of Vienna in 1815 to negotiate the end of the French revolutionary and Napoleonic Wars been asked what they expected of the next twenty-five years, virtually to a man the answer would have been something like this: "Another twenty-five years of continent-wide revolutionary violence and revolutionary war—or at least the ever-present threat of such disorder." In short, they expected the next twenty-five years to be much like the last twenty-five. What actually followed was one hundred years of relative peace, evolutionary rather than revolutionary changes, together with several wars which, while sometimes important, were nonetheless relatively short and limited, and not the violent, continent-wide, and long-drawn-out, and total struggles we associate with Napoleon and the French Revolution.

The most important thing that happened between 1815 and 1914 was that the industrial revolution spread from England to continental Europe. We can relate this to the first item on the chart of the "surprise-free projections"—to what we call the multifold trend—a trend which in most of its components or aspects goes back in Western culture some eight hundred to nine hundred years—although some of these aspects gain real force only in the last one hundred or two hundred years.

THE BASIC, LONG-TERM, MULTIFOLD TREND

1. Increasingly sensate (empirical, this-worldly, secular, humanistic, pragmatic, manipulative, explicitly rations, utilitarian, contractual, epicurean, hedonis-

tic, etc.) culture—recently an almost complete decline of the sacred and a relative erosion of "irrational" taboos, totems, charismas, and authority structures.

2. Bourgeois, bureaucratic, "meritocratic," and recently intellectual and technocratic elites.

3. Accumulation of scientific and technologic knowledge.

4. Institutionalization of technological change, especially research, development, innovation, and diffusion—recently and increasingly a conscious emphasis on new probability of synergisms and serendipities.

5. Worldwide industrialization and modernization.

6. Increasing capability for mass destruction.

7. Increasing affluence and (recently) leisure.

8. Urbanization and recently suburbanization and "urban sprawl"—soon the growth of megalopolises.

9. Population growth—now explosive but tapering off.

10. Decreasing importance of primary and (recently) secondary and tertiary occupations.

11. Increasing literacy and education—recently the "knowledge industry" and increasing numbers and roles of intellectuals.

12. Future-oriented thinking, discussion, and planning —recently some improvement in methodologies and tools—also some retrogression.

13. Innovative and manipulative rationality increasingly applied to social, political, cultural, and economic world—increasing problem of ritualistic, incomplete, or pseudo rationality.

14. Increasing universality of the multifold trend.

15. Increasing tempo of change in all the above.

This multifold trend is, I believe, an empirically observable fact. I would conjecture that nearly, but not quite, every Western historian would agree in general terms as to its existence and to the main features as set forth here. As for the historians who would deny it, some of the disagreement derives, I believe, from the same kind of problem we have when we try to ascertain the direction of flow of a river or even that there is a net flow in one direction. If you microscopically examine the river water, or observe it at a point close to the river mouth (and therefore encounter the phenomenon of tidal reversal) you may be unable to detect or verify the existence of an average direction of flow—even though the practical observation and even measurement of the phenomena is by no means difficult. The random fluctuations disclosed under the too-precise microscope, or the confusing forward and backward flows set up by the tides, are sufficient to obscure the major and—to another observer—obvious thing that is happening; a strong and continuing flow toward the sea. The observer must get away from microscopic scale and the tidal observation points, or average (with perhaps an impractical precision and objectivity) his observations over a period of time, to discover the general flow. I would guess that most, if not all of the historians who deny the existence of something like the multifold trend are misled by a "micro-scopic" concern with details or a parochial concern with special periods or special phenomena. But this last is by no means certain; despite my opinion there is certainly room for legitimate disagreement on this matter.

While we shall discuss this multifold trend again later, I might note here that its most interesting aspects is the trend toward increasingly sensate society. This is not just a question of an increasing role for science and-/or technology, but a systematic erosion of the sacred, of the role of taboos and totems, and in some ways even an erosion of the very concept of authority and tradition. It is obvious that there are many ebbs and flows in this "erosion of the sacred." One thinks of the Reformation and the Counter-Reformation, or the Enlightenment and the later Romantic Reaction. Further, many reli-gious humanists, some secular humanists, and many "cultists" would deny any formulation that attributed a lesser religiosity or sacredness to their personal beliefs. Making reasonable concessions to all of the above points of view, one can nevertheless argue persuasively that since the eleventh century or so there has been a general decrease in Western culture of the role of religion, and of sacred perspectives and attitudes, and an increase in the role of the mundane, the secular, the practical, and of humanist perspectives and attitudes. I personally would agree with many of the macrohistorians that this process may be the single most important aspect of the long-term multifold trend.

The first and most important assumption I am mak-ing about the next one or two decades is that the mul-tifold trend, which I believe to have been underway for the last eight or nine centuries, will continue, and probably accelerate—at least for a while. This assumption takes more courage than you might think. The multifold trend has had many ebbs and flows, and my conjecture is that it will largely flow and ebb very little during the next twenty years or so. (Though in a more complete exposition I could offer a score of scenarios—i.e., examples—on how there could be a "tidal reversal.")

But I also believe that this flow may change rather suddenly in character. To force the metaphor a little, toward the end of this century the river may cut a new river course which not only flows in a different direction but perhaps empties into a different sea. Thus, when in the "surprise-free projection" I refer to the onset of a postindustrial culture, I am suggesting that there will be a rather dramatic change in the nature of the multifold trend: a kind of "topping out" of some of its aspects, a halt or change in character in others, and even the generation of some new trends. It is like the Marxist argument that if something changes enough in quantity, such as by a slow decrease in the temperature of water, it eventually can become a dramatic qualitative change—the water becomes ice. I am suggesting that we are approaching as significant a qualitative point of change in our culture as any that has occurred in the history of civilized man.

When I later discuss the character of this change in our culture I will indulge myself by using some speakers' tricks to emphasize how dramatic the suggested change could be—that this change could indeed be one of the most dramatic events in history. I will also, in keeping with the assumed importance of this event use the most pretentious language of which I am capable.

The next item in the "surprise-free projection" concerns, among other things, the rise of Japan. Again we possess an analogy from the 1815–1914 time period. Alexis de Tocqueville's famous prediction in the 1830s of a coming struggle between the United States and Russia for world mastery, was widely accepted in his day, and stands up today as an extraordinary example of political insight and foresight. But we usually forget that if Germany had won World War I or II, Tocqueville's prediction would have been proven wrong. In 1870–71 there had been an event completely unexpected by Tocqueville: the rise of Prussia. This development could have wrecked almost any "surprise-free" projection of the future of Europe made in the first half of the nineteenth century. Actually, during the seventy-five years after 1871 the European system struggled to absorb the rise of Prussia, and this struggle, never wholly successful, still is unresolved today. Its legacy—today's divided Germany—is (as we suggest by including it in the "surprise-free projection") still potentially one of the explosive issues of the next decade or two.

I argue that the rise of Japan, say from 1970 on, provides an analogous event to the rise of Prussia. I am not predicting that a world war will result from it. Indeed, I would almost be willing to predict the opposite: that the net effect of this rise will be to increase stability against large war. I would also suggest that most people in the West and in the Third World will be helped, not hurt, by the rise of Japan—at least during the years which remain in this century. (But also note that I will only suggest this; I will not offer five to ten to one odds that this will be so.)

Let me review some recent history here. In the fifties, the Japanese economy grew, in real terms, by something more than a factor of two. This was an impressive but not unprecedented growth rate. In the sixties the Japanese economy grew by something more than a factor of three. This was unprecedented, particularly coming on top of the growth rate of the fifties. As a result of this rapid growth Japan passed West Germany and became the third largest economy in the world. It had started from something like the status of a Brazil or Argentina (to give a sense of the feat involved). There are a number of respectable estimates for the likely growth in the seventies. I believe that the lowest such estimate is a factor of 2.8, the highest is 4.5. I would argue that 3 to 4 is for our purposes a reasonable range to consider. Many experts on Japan are willing to say that such growth rates *may not* occur, giving many reasons for this belief; and they may be right. But almost no one asserts that they *will not* occur, at least no one who knows anything about Japan. This is quite a change. Let me add that these estimates of the Japanese growth rate allow for changes in the work force, and for large expenses for welfare, infrastructure, remaking the landscape, for control of pollution, for expansion of Japan's military establishment, and for other such issues.

At Hudson we flagged high Japanese growth rates as early as 1962–63 as being important and that, unlike the West German and Soviet cases, likely to be sustained for at least two decades, and thus as very important factors in our study of the long-term future. In 1962–63 this was only a plausible conjecture, but in 1966–67 we carried out a serious general study of the long-range prospects of Japan. The results of that study were published in my *The Emerging Japanese Superstate: Challenge and Response.* In that book I made three basic—and, I believe, high-confidence—arguments about Japan's likely rate of growth: (1) that the probabilities are very high that the Japanese growth rate will continue in the next two or three decades to greatly exceed the 5 per cent or so typical of the rest of the world, and indeed probably will exceed it by a factor of two or so; (2) that very likely the Japanese will attain the current U.S. per capita income ($5,000) by around 1980, and will catch up with the United States in per capita income by around 1990; (3) that by the year 2000 or so the Japanese GNP should be between 1.5 and 4.5 trillion (1970) dollars and thus may surpass the United States in total GNP, making Japan the largest economic power in the world. If not this they will at least very likely equal or pass the Soviet Union in GNP at that point, if they have not already done so earlier. In any case this will be an economic, financial, and technological superstate, and probably also a military and political superpower.

All of these are extremely important possibilities and have great potential political and psychological consequences as well as economic effects. The rest of my book on Japan, then, is concerned with various possible "challenges" and "responses" over the next decade or two to those Japanese growth rates. Thus when Japan doubled its economy in the fifties it just grew from small to medium—the impact on the world was small. When the economy tripled in the sixties the Japanese economy grew from medium to large—again the impact was small. But even if it grew by only a factor of three in the seventies, it will be growing from large to gigantic, and the impact will be very large. And even if there is a good deal of further tapering off in growth rates, the impact of the Japanese economy may be the most important issue which many corporations will have to face.

Let me cite some relatively dramatic economic examples that illustrate one of the issues. The United States in the early and mid-1960s had a fairly large industry manufacturing magnetic tape recorders for home entertainment and similar purposes. This industry has virtually disappeared; it has largely moved to Japan. We also had a fairly large radio industry; today it also has largely disappeared to the Far East, although not always to Japan. Today the United States has the largest television-manufacturing industry in the world. I do not know of anybody who believes that home-entertainment television sets will be manufactured in the United States in any great numbers in 1980. This production seems likely to go to Asia—not necessarily to Japan, but perhaps under American ownership or under American license to South Korea, Taiwan, or elsewhere. The current large phonograph and high-fidelity equipment industry in America also probably will move to Asia.

I recently gave a briefing in the United States to a major manufacturer of electrical equipment used for commercial communication. We looked over their list of products and I suggested that some 70 or 80 per cent would be manufactured in the Far East within the next ten years. One of the senior members of management stood up and declared, "Over my dead body." Another man then remarked that both positions were reasonable.

Now I happen to take quite seriously Adam Smith's

argument for free trade. I believe that from the absolute and domestic (but not the relative and/or internationally competitive) economic point of view Japan's growth will help, not hurt, the American economy. Indeed I would argue that the United States growth rate will be dragged up a half per cent or so because of the spectacular Japanese growth rate; maybe even a full percentage point. Canadian and Australian rates will also be pulled up—perhaps even more than the American. And there is likely to be a spectacular impact on certain parts of the Third World—particularly parts of Latin America and what might be called non-Communist Pacific Asia which will become increasingly involved with Japanese trade and investment. But if you happen to be among those business firms or industrial sectors which are hurt during the transition or adjustment stage, you may be very irritated.

On the political consequences of this rise of Japan I will say only this. There is another point of similarity to be noted with the rise of Prussia. By 1880, many Englishmen understood that Germany was likely to surpass Britain as the great industrial power of the world. On the whole, they were willing to accept this development, indeed to watch it with passive admiration. After all, the two countries were very close to each other. The British monarch was of German descent. Many Englishmen, at least among the aristocracy, had German relatives. The two aristocracies spent vacations in each other's homes; went to each other's schools. But in 1890, Kaiser Wilhelm II dismissed Bismarck. During the next ten years the Kaiser, in effect, worked as hard as he could—even if unintentionally—to embitter English-German relationships. He probably did not realize that he was doing this; but he succeeded. His biggest single mistake was the creation of a large German navy. There was no compelling reason for this. Germany needed the money and other resources for its army and industry. The Berlin-Baghdad railroad and German's economic and political drive to the East were going well, and with British toleration, if not blessing. But by challenging the Royal Navy's supremacy at sea, Germany drove the British into an entente with the French—their 400-year-old enemy. The World War I alignment of forces now was more or less inevitable, or at least I would argue so.

I think the big issue today between Japan and the United States, and indeed between Japan and the rest of the world, is not to re-create that kind of a situation. Today I believe the Americans, like the British a century ago, are pretty much willing to watch—and even encourage—the rise of Japan. When I discuss this issue in Washington I generally find that there is a certain feeling of pride in American government circles: "That's our protege!" Indeed, we Americans generally (with the obvious exceptions of certain chauvinists and of protection-minded businessmen and politicians), for reasons that are not entirely clear to me, often take great pride in this Japanese growth, as well as admiring it. I suspect we are basically correct to do so, and that the rise of Japan is more likely than not to be a good thing—both economically and politically—for the world. But I will not try to say more about this at this time.

The next aspect of the "surprise-free" projection is the coming "1985 technological crisis." This concept derives from an article which John von Neumann published in the mid-1950s arguing that the world is running out of room. Neumann contrasted the small size of the earth to the pollutant and other effects of man's new activities and new techniques and suggested 1980 as the year in which this problem would become dramatically apparent. I take this to mean a decade of crisis in the eighties—hence the term "1985 technological crisis"—and I will use the phrase to include other issues raised by technology than simply those involving the finite size of the earth. I must add that nothing has happened since 1955 to shake one's belief in the estimates made by von Neumann.

This threat was ranked somewhat further down on the versions of the surprise-free projections that I used in the mid- and late sixties. In discussing the point I would also often remark that one of the coming issues of politics would probably be pollution, and that the issue would be exaggerated. I thought that it would be very hard to exaggerate the pollution issue but that people would, in fact, succeed in doing so. This has occurred. One can hardly pick up a magazine today—and I speak of the least serious magazines, screen magazines, confession magazines, pulp magazines—without finding an article on pollution.

While the pollution issue is an important one, this concept of a 1985 technological crisis is much broader in scope. We have compiled a list of seventy potentially hazardous possibilities in the following seven areas: intrinsically dangerous technology; gradual degradation of environment; spectacular degradation of environment; dangerous internal political issues; upsetting international consequences; dangerous personal choices; and bizarre issues.[2] While I use the word "technological" in a very broad sense in listing those crises, none of those threats were frivolously listed or simply put down to extend the list. As far as we know today, any one of them could be associated, in the next decade or two, with enormous difficulties if not tragedies. Considering this list of relatively imminent technological dangers, it is hard to believe that we will cope successfully with all of them, though we might. Many, of course, may prove to be non-problems or non-issues. Consider the so-called contamination of the atmosphere by carbon dioxide as a result of our vast burning of fossil fuels. It is generally believed that there is considerably more carbon dioxide in the atmosphere than normal, and that the amount is likely to increase further by the end of the century. Calculations have been made that suggest we may find this producing a "greenhouse effect" that will, by the year 2000, be sufficient to melt a portion of the polar ice caps, perhaps raising the worldwide level of the oceans by five to ten feet. Others have suggested much more drastic changes. Still others have suggested that the whole effect is negligible. These calculations are very uncertain. Historically, most such predictions of worldwide effects have not been validated by events; but we simply do not know at the present time that this will continue to be true for many—not to say all—of the threats we include under the rubric "1985 technological crisis." Hence the typical —and to some degree justifiable—apocalyptic language.

There could, for example, be exactly the opposite disaster to the so-called greenhouse effect. One result of human activity has been to thrust up into the outer atmosphere a great amount of dust, of particulate matter.

These particles are often of such a size that they tend to reflect ultraviolet rays from the sun but rather freely let out the infrared radiated by the earth's surface; as a result, their presence acts to cool rather than heat the earth. Neumann made some interesting calculations on this phenomenon. He thought there could rather easily come about a pronounced cooling in the earth's temperature—perhaps even a new ice age. Again the calculations are very uncertain.

Let me give the most alarmist view of the issue, as it was put to me by a friend. Imagine you are building a Hollywood film set, and you want it to last until 1980. Somebody points out that the paint will have cracked by 1978. So you use a better paint. He points out that the concrete may also begin to crumble, so you put in more reinforcing rod and more cement and less sand. But he also points out that the plumbing will wear out in 1982. That does not bother you; you intend to abandon the set in 1980. The electrical wiring is estimated to wear out in 1988; this does not bother you either. You know you are going to abandon the set in 1980. In some ways the world today looks like that kind of a Hollywood set, designed—or at least currently operated—so as to be abandoned at some point in the early eighties.

While I would not accept this formulation as a wholly accurate estimate of current practices, I do believe that a Martian anthropologist examining current prospects could, with only a little bias in his analysis, make a remarkably persuasive case for the above diagnosis and prognosis. In any case, there is no question that some of the seventy or so technologically threatening issues I have listed will, if not corrected soon, dominate some aspects of our lives and endeavors during the next two or three decades. There are a number of reasons for this.

There is another important reason why some groups emphasize pollution issues. Such issues can have important political connotations. While they are issues on which the right, the left, and the center seem to find solid agreement, they share a special radiance for the left. In the past the left often talked about the "increasing immiseration of the masses," arguing the false or illusionary character of the seeming success of industrial society in general and of the benefits of modern affluence and technology in particular. In the middle and late twentieth century it has been increasingly difficult to make this position convincing. But the pollution issue now makes it possible. Rather than talk about the affluent society the left now talks about the *effluent* society; rather than talk about gross national product the left now talks about gross national *pollution.* As a result, a man of the left can argue that all this marvelous technology, all this unbelievable affluence created by industrialism and capitalism, has been unmasked, and that progress has proven to be only a complicated way to produce garbage, to destroy the ecology and landscape, and to dehumanize the individual. Thus the traditional negative picture of "progress" held by much of the left, and especially by today's new left, is regarded as having been validated.

If you are a man on the right, particularly in the United States, you are likely to be a hunter or a fisherman, an outdoors man, with a love of unpolluted streams, clear skies, and the like, an instinctive conservationist and enemy of environmental corruption. When

National Review, a conservative American magazine, recently published an article which attacked the anti-pollution movement as the product of a left-wing bias, it got a great deal of mail, most saying that the correspondent normally agreed wholeheartedly with the political views of the magazine, but on this matter he violently dissented.

Even the political center tends to hold strong views on pollution, agreeing with both left and the right on the desirability of pure and odorless water, clear air, and uncluttered landscapes. We appreciate the threats to human survival which pollution poses. Indeed one can make a good case that it is wise to overstate this issue. Generally speaking, there are two kinds of mistakes to make: to fail to convict the guilty, or to convict the innocent—i.e., one can fail to act when one should; or act when one should not. Normally, it is arguable which is the more serious mistake to make. You do not want emotion to cloud these issues, because emotion is dangerously biased. On pollution, it is often (but not always) different. If government or society overreacts, or reacts when it should not, there will be some waste of resources and some unnecessary—and perhaps temporary—interference with useful or pleasurable activities. Normally this will be no tragedy. But if there is a failure to act when action should be taken, then an important ecological resource or balance—a river, a forest, a reservoir, or other asset—may be irrevocably lost. Faced with the possibility of such irrecoverable loss, most people, looking at the two kinds of mistakes, vote to take the chance of excessive, too rapid, or too strong a governmental reaction as the better mistake to make. One can sympathize with that; at least if one is not the individual or organization whose interests are at stake. As a result, the increasing emphasis on environmental issues is likely to make an increasing difference to the operations and activities of both individuals and of business. Indeed, this is just one aspect of what we now call "consumerism" in the United States—an emphasis on the collective rights, desires, and welfare of the consumers and general public.

Arguments on pollution can become very emotional, sometimes with unexpected overtones. For example, someone has calculated that the temperature of New York City is some five degrees hotter in the summer because of the ejection of heat by air-conditioning equipment. The issue could be formulated as a matter of the rich ejecting heat (i.e., excreting the waste products of the air-conditioner) upon the people in the street and on the poor who do not possess air-conditioning. If this last were completely true it could become a very bitter political issue, but luckily in New York City a good many of the poor also have air-conditioning. But in any case it is clear that you may be able to tolerate a five-degree increase in the heat of the city streets, but you cannot allow many doublings of this increase. You just do not want ten or twenty degrees extra summer heat for those without—or outside—air-conditioning.

But as I have indicated, the coming "1985 technological crisis" includes many kinds of issues other than pollution—some of which will be discussed later. I also want to suggest why this potential crisis in our society has such a profound political, moral, morale, and psychological effect on many upper-class and upper-middle-class young people. This relates to the fifth issue on the basic "surprise-free projection." Among other things we are concerned here with value issues, with the problem of the new "search for meaning and purpose"; and with some of the cultural and value confusions that are so prominent today. Though these issues are, in a way, the main subject of this presentation, I am not able to spend very much time on them—that is, specifically on what the value changes are that are occurring, why they are occurring, and what they might mean. Bell has already mentioned that the politics of 1975–85 will very likely be different from today. Politics will be less about the distribution of shares of GNP than about ideological issues, about the good life, about what is meant by a decent and healthy human life, what one means by a humanistic philosophy. Let me begin with what I call "The Twelve Traditional Societal Levers," as listed below:

THE 12 TRADITIONAL SOCIETAL "LEVERS"
(I.E., TRADITIONAL SOURCES OF "REALITY TESTING,"
SOCIAL INTEGRATION, AND/OR MEANING AND PURPOSE)

1. Religion, tradition, and/or authority.

2. Biology and physics (e.g., pressures and stresses of the physical environment, the more tragic aspects of the human condition, etc.).

3. Earning a living or even concur with the "five guarantees."

4. Defense of frontiers (territoriality).

5. Defense of vital strategic and economic interests.

6. Defense of vital political, moral, and morale interests.

7. The "martial" virtues such as duty, patriotism, honor, heroism, glory, courage, etc.

8. The manly emphasis—in adolescence: team sports, heroic figures, aggressive and competitive activities, rebellion against "female roles;" in adulthood: playing an adult male role (similarly a womanly emphasis).

9. The "Puritan ethic" (deferred gratification, work orientation, achievement orientation, advancement orientation, sublimation of sexual desires, etc.).

10. A high degree (perhaps almost total) of loyalty, commitment and/or identification with nation, state, city, clan, village, extended family, secret society, and/or other large grouping.

11. Other sublimation and/or repression of sexual, aggressive, aesthetic, and/or "other instincts."

12. Other "irrational" and/or restricting taboos, rituals, totems, myths, customs, and charismas.

In the past, with some exceptions, these levers have been somewhat more important in the United States— at least in the middle of the twentieth century, than in most of the rest of the world. Today, at least as far as the young people in the prestige universities in the United States are concerned, these are now largely eroded. This erosion of "traditional societal levers" is often taken as a generation gap, and to some degree it is. But it is actually more of a class than a generation gap. In the late fifties, the beatniks and the very early hippies and New Left radicals did tend to break with their parents almost completely, but current studies indicate that today, at least in the United States, the parents get along quite well not only with the hippies but with the radical young in the universities. This has been more of a shift by parents than the young people. It is really part and parcel of what Margaret Mead calls a "prefigurative culture" with the young learning from the old (as opposed to the cofigurative culture in which the young learn from their peer groups, and the postfigurative culture or traditional culture in which the young learn from the elderly). As a result there is a very big gap between upper and lower middle class in the United States, or sometimes between what we call progressive middle class and traditional middle class. This gap can be characterized by saying that to the traditional middle class the central issues of public, and to some degree private, life tend still to re-volve around the twelve traditional societal levers. These twelve societal levers rarely have any particular impor-tance or relevance to the more advanced members of the progressive middle class. Major change in eight or nine of the twelve levers probably means a long-term change, in the conditions and environment of the upper middle class—and one which it is hard to imagine being re-versed. Thus the change in values that results from deemphasizing these particular traditional societal levers reflects, as much as anything, a change in the "real world," and to that extent is not likely to be reversed by any normal or fortuitous political or other event—though, of course, intense pressures or issues could re-verse them. This is not so true of the erosion of the other three or four societal levers. Change there probably also has a relatively permanent character—at least as far as the upper middle class is concerned—but is much more subject to contingent historical events. (For example, the recent tightening of the job market has had some effect on the current crop of college graduates.)

It should be noted that the particular way these traditional societal levers are listed allows for some overlap and indistinctness of categories. I did this in order to be able to emphasize easily and conveniently the various points that I usually make in a much longer presentation. The attitudes and values one associates with an emphasis on the issue of "earning a living" is still one of the most significant of the societal levers. But to a startling degree —at least in the United States—people in the upper middle class no longer think of this as a major issue, much less the major issue, of their life. They assume that they can earn between $10,000 to $50,000 a year with little effort, and that this is largely sufficient for their needs, and they also know that with even moderate efforts they probably can make money at the upper end of this range. They may even choose to drop out completely and live as a hippie. I should note here that the hippie is almost exclusively an upper-middle-class (or progressive-middle-class) movement. In 1968, a series of surveys on what it cost to live as a hippie suggested that about $10 a week or $500 a year was required. This meant that upper-middle-class kids who often were, in some sense, playing at being poor, could live twelve to a pad and work one month in the post office and take eleven off. (The U.S. post office at that time paid a minimum salary of $500 a month, just enough to supply all the needs of a little community of twelve hippies where each one took a turn in earning the monthly requirement. Since these kids are all relatively literate, they do well in the postal-service examination, scoring well above their less literate and less well-educated poor or lower-middle-class competitors.)

Take the traditional lever of defending frontiers. Canada and Sweden both spend a great deal each year on defense. Would one of these countries feel any safer if it doubled its expenditure? No. Would they feel any more endangered if they halved it? No. I happen to think there are very good reasons for both countries to spend that money, but I do not know that I am right. It would have to be a complicated argument. In any case, the simple feeling that a nation with more defense is safer has disappeared. Costa Rica has recognized this and disbanded its army.

Now, I would argue there are many reasons for defense in this rather strange world of ours, but they are complicated and controversial; they are not simple and straightforward. Take vital strategic and economic interests. If you use the word "vital" to mean a matter of life and death, the United States has no vital economic or strategic interests in any part of the world outside its own territory. I am prepared to take a contract to design a military/economic policy for the United States to retreat to the fifty states and defend itself against the combined might of the rest of the world, including even Canada and Latin America. I will be able to argue that a very high standard of living could be maintained and, except for some issues with regard to the arms race, Americans need not necessarily feel much less secure than they feel today. If this position is correct, then clearly the United States has no vital, strategic or economic interests anywhere in the world. I have made this statement before many military groups and, after we go over it, they generally just say "yes."

Now, in my judgment, there are many vital political, moral, and morale interests for the American nation. But if I say this to young people in a prestige college, they think I am saying that I am willing to risk tens of millions of American lives for the difference between chocolate ice cream and vanilla. In general, the young at prestige universities do not understand such value issues—or at least they reject them.

Let me now tell another short anecdote about Israel that will further illustrate what I mean by the reality testing of the societal levers. About 40 per cent of Israeli Jews are of European extraction, the rest being of oriental origin. Jews of European extraction are typically fairer, taller, better educated, and richer than those from North Africa or the Middle East. The European Jews run the country and are almost forcibly Europeanizing the oriental Jews as rapidly as possible. Every now and then an oriental Jew will go up to a European Jew and say, "I don't like your European bourgeois values. What you are doing to me is cultural aggression. Leave me alone." The European Jew answers, "We are surrounded by a hundred million Arabs." The oriental Jew thinks for about ten seconds and then asks, very reluctantly, "Where is the engineering school?" He has no other choice. I want to emphasize here how the need for defending frontiers straightened this individual out in two different ways. First, no matter what his real value systems are, they must include sufficient European values to enable him to learn engineering or he is in serious trouble. In fact, he won't survive. Secondly, if one checks, one ordinarily would find that this oriental youth was not really expressing a deeply held position. He was expressing a current fashion and a certain amount of frustration and annoyance. The reality testing forced him to think through his own position more clearly.

I am not arguing here that European value systems are going to be everywhere preeminent. In fact, I believe that the opposite is true, that worldwide, both inside and outside of the Western culture we will find a revolt against traditional European values. I am arguing that as far as this Israeli is concerned the chances are almost overwhelming that he prefers European value systems to some or all of his traditional values. The point of the twelve societal levers is that they do force one to check with reality. Thus, if one is interested in earning a living, and acts foolishly, he is fired or fails to be promoted. Or a lack of realism on another issue may cause his country to be invaded, or to lose a vital interest of some sort. Religion can also encourage reality testing, in the sense that one feels a shock to one's conscience or shame or some other reaction if the tenets are violated. Yet to a degree which still tends to astonish many Americans of my age, none of the items on the above list has any serious significance for a large per cent of those Americans who attend elite universities, and to some degree for the upper middle class generally—particularly those under thirty. They simply will not compromise, or exert an extra effort, in order to conform to the requirements of this list.

I now want to comment on the decline of the Puritan ethic. Leo Szilard once contrasted what he felt was a literary approach to issues as opposed to a scientific approach. The literary person tends to ask, "Who said it?"

"Why did he say it?" "Why now?" In the scientific approach one asks, "What did he say?" "Is it right?" At this point I would like to take what Szilard called the literary approach, and ask the questions of *who, why,* and *why now.*

When I make talks at American universities, I often try to divide my audience into two groups, an upper-middle-class group and a lower-middle-class group. After doing this, I then ask the upper-middle-class group to search their entire lives to find any reasonable request which they have ever made for some object or goal which they did not realize within a year or so. Now to want a yacht at the age of ten is not a reasonable request, but to want a bike at the age of ten is reasonable. Indeed, for these Americans to want a car at eighteen, a motorboat at nineteen, or a trip to Paris at twenty-one are all reasonable.

Let me now discuss the results of this poll. Remarkably, often no hands or just one or two hands may be raised. Most or all of the group feels that, by and large, all their reasonable desires had been satisfied within a year. There are many reasons for this feeling. One of them is the American orgy of gift giving every Christmas and every birthday. Twice a year the parents get together and ask in desperation, "What can we get the little monster that he doesn't already have?" Generally, when they have finished their own creative thinking on this problem, the grandmother or some other relative comes along and adds substantially to the kid's loot. As a result, many young Americans have, for all practical purposes, been denied the experience of having to wait two or more years for something they wanted. Now this is a bit of exaggeration; most of these Americans have spent long years trying to get into college and working very hard to do it. But the *attitude* I'm trying to indicate is not an exaggeration. For example, in the 1968 campaign, Senator Eugene McCarthy had about twenty thousand young people working with him. Some of them worked about two months, some of them worked about six months. When he reached Oregon he had about eight thousand of these young people with him, and they formed one of the most fantastically effective political organizations ever seen. In fact, these young people were remarkably effective campaigners in almost every part of the country. They were so effective they almost took over a major political party. Now if that had happened to my age group I think we would have been really elated. We would have said, "My God, we almost did it, in just two to six months of trying. Next year in Jerusalem!" We would have been unbelievably impressed with our capability, buoyed up by our near-success.

As far as I can tell—and I spent a fair amount of time with these young people—nothing like this occurred. Almost to a man they seemed to have cried "fraud." Now they were not referring to the little frauds that actually occurred around the country in various election places, but to the basic fraud, in their judgment, that the system must be corrupt because they could not take the Democratic Party over in less than six months. They really felt there must be something basically wrong if it took longer than that to achieve their objectives.* This is indeed the "now generation" in a number of ways, most important of which is that they face all kinds of critical issues which

---

*And in 1972, they succeeded in taking over the Democratic Party.

simply cannot be solved in less than a decade or two decades. But this group insists on immediate, dramatic, and total solution.

Recently I got a lot of mail and telephone calls from friends strongly urging me to use whatever influence I had to oppose the American move into Cambodia and to promote a precipitous American withdrawal from Vietnam. Many of these people knew that I have been studying these problems for many years, have very strong opinions on the subject, and I have a reputation for speaking out as I feel. It is very strange that they would think such pleas would change my mind. Their position was that the young people were desperate. The students have tried everything, and nothing yet has worked, and therefore they will no longer wait. They insisted to me that the young people had tried every peaceful method of achieving their goal, and now nothing was left but bombs or revolution. My uniform reply to these people was, "If that is so, they've lost, and that's all there is to it." It is interesting that few if any adults tried to give these young people any sense of proportion.

There is nothing in the American system that says that those who lose have an obligation to escalate. It's the nature of the system that those who lose accept their loss, and go back and try again. Now, if I shared the young peoples' judgment on the U.S. Government, I would feel morally obligated to go outside the system. In fact if I shared their views about Vietnam I would have done so a long time ago. But I don't share their beliefs. I don't think they do themselves. This is one of the reasons why they have to justify themselves so much when they talk of going outside the system.

The issue of "the new political milieu" on the "surprise-free projection" is a fairly broad one. It can be used to refer to the fact that the Soviet Union is beginning to have a situation in which, as opposed to the prewar situation, the government probably has the loyalty and trust of the average worker and the average farmer, but has lost part of the managerial class and the intellectuals. The exact opposite was true prewar, and, while the change has been gradual, it now seems to have been accomplished. If so, then that is a different political milieu. Or we might be referring to the fact that worldwide communism is, relatively speaking, low in morale, and that fact changes the worldwide political milieu. We can, of course, point out that Western culture has even lower morale, and that to the extent that the two ideologies are competitors it is perhaps the relative morale that counts —or perhaps not.

There are many new political milieus to be talked about. As far as I am concerned the most important new political milieu is the one that I think is going to develop in the United States. This is a kind of repetition of the 1920–40 political atmosphere, but much intensified. But let me deal with this in the course of my remarks on the later items in our projection.

My projection suggests that worldwide law-and-order issues are going to be increasingly important for a long time to come—at least until the inevitable reaction comes. The reaction can come in many different forms, perhaps like the current U.S. reaction toward what we can call ideological renewal. Many people call this a right-wing movement or they think of it as a southern or racist movement, but both are at least partly wrong. It is simply one of the things suggested in the issue of populist and/or conservative backlashes and revolts. Later on, when I talk about trained incapacity, I will come back to this issue.

There recently was a time when we were told by every articulate paper in America and almost all the scholars that "law and order" was a code phrase for anti-Negro sentiments. Does anybody believe that today? The Democratic party now understands that unless it picks law and order as its top issue, it is dead. By the way, in many American cities the Negroes picked law and order as the top issue of the 1968 campaign.

Or take "backlash"—how many people have heard the term used as implying a rising animosity and prejudice against blacks? How many people believe this exists? There is no evidence of such backlash; indeed all the evidence goes the other way. There have been literally hundreds of polls on this issue. There do not seem to be any that contradict the point that I am about to make: Lower-middle-class America is traditionally anti-Negro. With unbelievable rapidity they are losing their anti-Negro sentiments. Every year they seem to be less anti-Negro. Even in complex polls asking such questions as "Are you for welfare?" the answer is usually "yes," even though welfare is often a pseudonym for Negro. A Gallup poll I saw two or three months ago is typical. In 1963 61 per cent of white southern parents said they would not send their children to a school with even a small number of Negroes. Only 16 per cent take that position today.

It is interesting to note that *Newsweek*, which may have the best data available on Negroes, had a whole issue on Negroes which had a page or so on backlash which their own data showed did not exist. *Time* magazine also had an issue which emphasized Negro issues. Their data also showed that the backlash did not exist, but they devoted a half page to it. By and large upper-middle-class Americans cannot read their own polls, and if they do read them, can't absorb them.

There is a backlash, but it is of a quite different kind. Indeed, it is building up today with very great emotional intensity. For the first time in U.S. history we have a nationwide populist revolt on our hands. Always before we had only regional populist revolts; now it's country-wide. The so-called "middle American" is very upset. But his revolt is largely against upper-middle-class America—not against blacks. It is against a very specific set of intellectuals—the ones that advise the government and write for the minority or scholarly press, or otherwise publish liberal ideology, often under the guise of objective reporting or objective scholarship. Upper-middle-class America likes to believe the backlash is racism. They don't want to believe that the problem is asserted to be themselves. Indeed this possibility has almost never occurred to them. Mayor Lindsay of New York is just beginning to catch on to this. Several of his spokesmen admitted that they knew nothing about middle America until about 1969. This statement is obviously correct, but it is unexpected to find it made in public. While John Lindsay is the mayor of the second largest city in the world and one which is roughly three-quarters lower-middle class—or middle America—he was largely a candidate of WASPs, Jews, Negroes, and the upper and upper middle class.

Let me go on to the next issue—the general decrease in consensus and authority. This is probably the most important issue from the practical point of view, but from the ideological point of view it may seem to amount to more of the same. Authority has nothing to do with power, wisdom, or knowledge. The use of power is coercion, not authority, and the use of wisdom or knowledge is persuasion or subversion, not authority. Authority is simply the right to, say, suggest, or order something, and to be listened to seriously simply because the "author" has authority. As Hannah Arendt has said, the essence of authority is that the exerciser has it because he has it. Throughout most of history someone usually had authority in this sense. Some cultures emphasized it enormously (Roman). Some cultures never really understood it (Greek), and kept searching for it because, so to speak, they needed it to make the system work. The family is the last stronghold of authority. If the parent does not understand authority, nobody will. Why is this important? In some sense Western culture started to erode in the twenties and thirties in ways that I don't want to discuss now, but authority largely remained. That authority seems to have eroded in the sixties, some thirty years later. It wasn't particularly noticed, but the practical impact is large.

This decreasing sense of authority, I believe, comes directly out of the multifold trend, but may also be a necessary prelude to the postindustrial culture. One effect, I believe, will be the creation of what I call a "mosaic society." Mosaic here means a pattern with many enclaves. Perhaps 80 to 90 per cent of the people may be in some sense "square," but there are likely to

be important groups who "do their own thing," espous-
ing their own values, attitudes, dress, language, work,
institutions, etc. If you go to the University of California
in Berkeley today you can almost tell what school the
students are in by how they dress. Roughly, engineering
and business dress "square," physicists dress in half
shirtsleeves, half dress–half work pants; math students
for some reason or other tend to dress like "Hell's An-
gels," complete with leather belt and leather jacket; psy-
chology and sociology students are often hippie, complete with beads and amulets. I suspect Berkeley is a
microcosm of part of our future.

Let us now go back and review the first issues in the
basic "surprise-free projection" in the light of what I
have said about the whole picture. We start with the first
point, the multifold trend. Anything that has been going
on for eight or nine centuries should have been noticed
by now. If you have not noticed it you probably have not
been awake. Therefore there should not be anything
particularly startling in that list. In addition, much of this
material in this list was covered in Dr. Bell's papers.
Indeed I could probably summarize most of his talk,
perhaps unfairly, by suggesting that he spent most of his
time on several of those points. I believe he went deep
enough and well enough into all of these issues so that
there is no need for me to add anything here on these
subjects, except for some disagreements in substance or
emphasis. However, if I was asked to pick out the most
important trend on this chart, I think I would pick out the
long-term secular trend as the dominating, if often un-
recognized—and therefore implicit—issue. Indeed, recently there has been an almost unbelievable decline in

—and erosion of—the sacred, the traditional, and the concept of authority—at least among the upper and upper-middle classes of the United States, much of Western Europe, and much of Latin America. In some ways Sweden is a leader in this movement, and in some ways it is not. In Sweden there are certain reality tests and sources of social unity that other Western countries, particularly the larger ones, do not have.

When I talk about the decline of the sacred, I am talking about a process which has gone so far that the issues are now quite foreign to modern secular man; so foreign that it is hard to describe what one means. It is a little bit like discussing relativity theory with an audience that has not had elementary physics. They lack the background for simple explanation. Just to give you an example of what I mean—my grandfather literally walked with God. He woke up in the morning, obtained his instructions, carried them out, and discussed the results in the evening. Now, he had a very different view of the world from ours. Among other things, he had a sense of identity and a kind of personal confidence that is still impressive to me. Let me contrast his attitude with those that are common today. Take for example the recent Papal Encyclical on birth control: it has been said that this could not be good church dogma because the acceptance of this position was likely to increase human unhappiness; therefore, it simply was not an acceptable position. This argument was raised almost everywhere. My grandfather would not have accepted this formulation. Rather he would have replied to this position, "What else is new?" The idea that one judges religious dogma by criteria of human happiness would have struck him as an oddity—or even an amusing absurdity. I refer you to the Book of Job for the argumentation for this position. In fact, one can argue that this formulation of the issue—assuming that morality and human happiness, or morality and practical utility to mankind, or even morality and human welfare, are related to each other—only goes back a few hundred years in recent Western culture. We are told by some historians that there is no scrap of paper that has come down to us from the early Middle Ages (that is, from the sixth to the tenth century) which refers to human happiness. The subject simply was not of interest, at least to those people who wrote.

The second aspect of the multifold trend—the rise of the bourgeoisie—has more than a passing connecting with the point that Dr. Bell made about the increasing role of the technocrat. To some degree, these technicians are beginning to inherit the role of the bourgeois —government by the bourgeois is becoming more and more replaced by government by technocratic bureaucracies. The reasons for this development were also discussed by Dr. Bell, as were also other aspects of the increasing power and role of technology, the importance of knowledge elites, and the increasing role of futuristic thinking. I need not say anything further about those issues here. I would, however, like to add something to Dr. Bell's remarks about occupational change. In pointing out the decreasing role of primary and secondary occupations and activities he referred to the increasing importance of tertiary activities. I would like to make a distinction here and call "tertiary" only those activities that are basically services to primary and secondary activities or services to such services. I would also like to define a different kind of activity that might be thought of as "quaternary" activities. A quaternary activity is something that is not essential to sheer survival and is either done for its own sake—for example, certain kinds of play or education—or services to such services. For example, air travel today is a relatively quaternary activity, since about 60 per cent of all passengers are traveling on personal business not related to private or government business. It is believed that this percentage may grow much larger by the end of the century. I prefer thinking of the postindustrial culture as a culture in which quaternary activities are dominant. You might ask, what difference does it make if one supplies services to a sculptor, or a skier, or to a man in the construction or the manufacturing business? Many of us believe that it makes a great deal of difference.

One way to look upon this is to note that a quaternary or postindustrial culture is very far removed from the Chinese concept of "the five guarantees": adequate food, adequate clothing, adequate shelter, adequate medical care, and adequate funeral expenses—all adequate by Chinese standards. Quaternary criteria are simply not deeply concerned with the five guarantees—at least as the Chinese view this concept.

This trend, which reaches its limits in the postindustrial culture (in which the primary, secondary, and tertiary occupations become of almost trivial importance), is today of importance in all countries—even ones that are very distant from being postindustrial. However, it is only those that are close to postindustrial in which the "knowledge industry" dwarfs all other industries. This does not mean that you may not have an inordinately large role for intellectuals in even relatively primitive countries. India, for example, has a serious problem of unemployed college students. But it is only in the postindustrial or near-postindustrial societies that the dominant group of people make their living, in some form or another, from the knowledge industry. And the intellectuals (people who deal mainly with ideas—and who derive their experience of the world in a second-hand manner, and who often attempt to idealize or intellectualize issues) become a numerous or even dominant group as a result of their sheer numbers.

We include in the trend the idea of progress and the revolution of rising expectations. This has resulted, of course, in the twentieth century in deliberate and planned economic development. We also note that there has been some regression in our ability to plan our future—in part because the modern intellectual tends to be educated mainly in relatively technical or technological fields and lacks a sense of history; in part because he lacks certain kinds of practical experience; and, finally, and perhaps most important, because in the late sixties many people accepted studies uncritically while in the late fifties they tended to be skeptical if not hostile. In any case the quality of the people doing the planning today may not be as high as was common ten to twenty years ago. Nevertheless, this is the age of innovative and manipulative rationality increasingly applied to the social, political, cultural, and economic worlds, as well as to shaping and exploiting the material world. This, in turn, seems to bring with it increasing problems of ritualistic, incomplete or pseudo rationality—e.g., a rationality whose job is less to give objective guidance than to satisfy certain bureaucratic, morale, public relations, or other ritualistic or psychological demands and needs— some of which, of course, are important and legitimate.

The last elements of the multifold trend are now obvious; many of us are now beginning to believe that these two at least must top out—that the multifold trend can no longer be increasingly worldwide and with an increasing tempo of change both within and outside of Western culture.

Let me now return to the second major trend on our Basic Surprise-Free Projection, the onset of the Post-Industrial culture, or more accurately, let me reexamine what I like to call the Emergent U.S. Year 2000 Postindustrial Culture. Except for some differences in emphasis and some conjectures, the chart describes much the same phenomenon that Bell discussed.

THE "EMERGENT U.S. YEAR-2000" POSTINDUSTRIAL
(OR POST-MASS-CONSUMPTION) SOCIETY

1. Most "economic" activities are quaternary (largely personal and self-serving, services to such activities, or services to such services) rather than primary, secondary, or tertiary (oriented toward production and distribution of goods).

2. Per capita income $5,000 to $25,000/year (or about ten times industrial and a hundred times preindustrial).

3. Narrow economic "efficiency" no longer primary.

4. Market may play diminished role compared to public sector and "social accounts."

5. Official floor on income and welfare for "deserving poor"—effective floor for others.

6. There may be more "consentive" and anarchic type organizations (vs. "marketives and "command systems").

7. Business firms may no longer be the major source of innovation or center of attention.

8. Widespread use of automation, computers, cybernation.

9. Small world—"global metropolis" not "global village."

10. Typical "doctrinal lifetime" two to twenty years.

11. Learning society—emphasis on late knowledge, imagination, courage, and innovation—deemphasis of experience, judgment, caution, and perhaps wisdom.

12. Rapid improvement in institutions and techniques for training and teaching—"education" may lag.

13. Erosion (in some upper and upper middle classes) of work-oriented, achievement-oriented, advancement-oriented, deferred-gratification values.

14. Likely erosion (at least in these same classes) of the other eleven "traditional levers" as search for "meaning and purpose."

15. Much apparent "late sensate chaos and polarization."

16. Sensate, secular, humanist, perhaps self-indulgent criteria may become central in important groups—at least during this transition period.

17. But the search for "meaning and purpose" will largely find at least an interim solution (or solutions).

18. This solution may contain important elements that are "against progress," against numbers 15 and 16 above, and/or against rationality and/or "Western culture."

I suggested earlier that I would use the most pretentious language of which I was capable when discussing this postindustrial revolution. Let me start with a rhetorical trick. If you ever want to impress an audience, one way is to use very large numbers. Refer to the fact that there are a hundred billion stars in the galaxy. How many people normally count that high? If that is not sufficient, point out that there are a hundred billion galaxies in the universe. That is impressive. Or, you might say that man has been on earth for two million years. How many studies look back that far when they start? Very few. All right, let me employ the trick.

Man has been on earth now for two million years. I have examined every one of those years rather carefully. I have noticed only two events of any interest. The rest is trivia, an unbelievable amount of trivia! However, I ought to be a little careful. If you are a religious individual, you will want to add a third event to the two which I am about to discuss. But we might disagree as to what that third event is (I am referring, of course, to the Covenant of God with Abraham). I gather that some of you would not agree or even understand. Let us therefore leave this religious event out of the discussion completely, and just discuss the two secular events on which we can all agree and take equally seriously.

Let me attempt to give an encapsulated description of man's past economic history together with a look at his future. The first stage of man's productive culture— hunting or food gathering—lasted for the first million years or so of his existence. It is difficult to compute per capita income in this mode of production but we can argue that, depending upon circumstances, it was something between $50 and $250 per capita, fully understanding that this is a nearly impossible kind of estimate to make. About ten thousand years ago occurred the first of the two past great events I'm going to talk about—the agricultural revolution. It started in the so-called Fertile Crescent of the eastern Mediterranean and launched civilization. Civilization means civic culture, living in cities, and some but not all of the early agricultural societies created such a manner of living. For every ten, twenty, or thirty people on the farm there was one man in the city. Very likely the average per capita income did not change, remaining something between $50 and $250 per year. What did change, of course, was the density of population and the way of life.

Indeed, as far as we know, no culture ever went much over $250 per capita in individual income or ever dropped much below $50 until the industrial revolution in the eighteenth century. This was the second great event of history, as we are looking at it, and it eventually changed per capita income by a factor of ten or so. We will as a matter of definition think of Europe in the 1950s as an instance of mature industrial culture. Southern Europe in the 1950s had about $500 per capita income, northern Europe about $2,500. However, in some ways we are less interested in per capita income than in the general style of life, the culture, and its capabilities.

We now understand that the next ten, twenty, or thirty years or so are likely to bring as big a change in man's condition as these first two: the emergence of postindustrial culture. Income again is expected to go up by about another factor of ten, but we are less interested in income than in the impact on styles of life and on our culture. By the year 2000 about 20 per cent of the world's population should be living in countries with an income at least within the postindustrial range.

Two other points are worth noting. The first is what I call the emergence of "almost post-economic" society. This is by no means a ridiculous concept. If per capita income continues to rise by 2.3 per cent or more a year (this is not a very startling rate of growth) then in a hundred years or so we should increase by another factor of ten in per capita income. This would mean 50,000 to 250,000 per capita per year. It seems reasonable to call this post-economic. Economic issues as we currently understand them are likely to be considered trivial or irrelevant. There will, of course, always be a problem of scarcity, and there will always be projects which people will be interested in doing which will have to be rejected because of their use of scarce resources, or at least in principle this should happen. But insofar as the standard economic issues which worry people today are concerned, one can call this a post-economic society. It should probably be added that a good deal written today about the post-industrial culture would in my opinion apply more to this virtually post-economic culture than to the kinds of conditions we expect to see in the late twentieth and early twenty-first centuries. The differences which will develop during the next thirty years are simply not that big.

In principle at least, economic growth could continue indefinitely,[3] and it gets more and more difficult to measure things like gross national product as we go into a "post-economic economy;" but in any case we should not forget that growth may continue well into the twenty-third and twenty-fourth centuries and beyond. Certainly it is difficult to imagine a society with wealth several hundred times our own. It may be postcivilized, it may be post-economic, it may be what we can call "truly human," or it may be post-human. That is, there may be people, but people made in a laboratory, or people who are half human, half artificial as is considered in the so-called cyborg concept; or it might be that human beings will be replaced by the computer, as has been suggested in science fiction. Instead we will return to the "Emergent U.S. Year-2000" post-industrial culture as the only topic that is really relevant to the future of the corporation in the seventies and the eighties.

It seems to me that the points in this list pretty well describe what is going on in the United States today—at least insofar as the current turmoil and some of the other changes are mainly related to the onset of this post-industrial culture. One can now assert, with some insistence, that by the end of the century the first two points will be realized, and very likely the third as well.

But in discussing this third point I have a problem. I do not want to identify myself with those who think that there is so much plenty and affluence in the world that efficiency is not at all important. But I do want to argue that the marginal value of economic efficiency, narrowly defined, has decreased in our society, will decrease further in the future, and probably should do so—although perhaps not to the degree which many argue.

In the United States before 1930, when an American applied for a job he usually asked only two questions: "What is the salary?" and "What are the chances for advancement?" This is one of the reasons why our country grew so fast. You could literally move a man from New England to southern California for an extra five cents an hour. You could not move him back, but that did not make too much difference, since the net migration was the other way. But this is no longer true. Today the typical American asks a number of questions. For example, "What are the fringe benefits?" "What do you do or make?" (It is much easier to hire a man for something interesting and significant.) "What kind of an organization are you?" "What kind of people do you produce?" "How are decisions made?" "Will I really enjoy working in that kind of place?" "Will I mature?" "Will I exercise most of my skills?" These are almost unbelievable questions to any man who is used to the old-fashioned American. The typical American still asks, and this is sometimes overlooked, "What is the salary?" "What are the chances for advancement?" Today it is considered indecent to sacrifice your family or your friends or almost anything else for salary and advancement. Let me elaborate this point because it really is a central change.

If you ever want to find the true feelings of the people, to understand what is going on in their hearts, look at their third-class literature. Today these are the soap operas, the confession magazines, the grade C movies, and so on. None of these are confused by genius or creativity. They speak from the cliché heart to the cliché heart. Studies of these media have been done. Let me give you some interesting results. Take the soap opera. In 1930, whenever there was a conflict between job and family or between advancement and friendship, job and advancement always won out or there was a tragedy. In 1960, when the same conflict arose (unless the job was altruistic, like a doctor, a psychiatrist, or the director of the Hudson Institute) family won out, or there was a tragedy. In 1930, an American who earned a million dollars and picked up an ulcer in the process was looked upon as a hero, wounded in the battle for success, and deserving of greater honor than the millionaire who did not have an ulcer—i.e., who was not wounded. In 1960, that same man was portrayed as a compulsive neurotic with twisted values. He is sick; send him to the hospital.

I recently gave a lecture on this topic to an organization of young men who are presidents of their own business firms. One member of the audience got very upset and complained, "No, no, that's only true of what you call the humanist left. No one else thinks that way—at least no reasonable man would react that way." So I polled the young business presidents that were there. Of about sixty people, all but two agreed that the man was sick.

Sometimes a businessman asks me, "Who pays for this society of yours?" I generally answer, "Business. So what?" Now you may remember my earlier comment that in earlier civilizations there were twenty or so people on the farm for every man in the city. Today the United States is postagricultural—3 per cent or so produce more than 95 per cent of the foods and fibers we need and they could double their production if we asked them to. Agriculture does not take much percentage of our society. I ask, "Have you recently—or ever—felt a spasm of gratitude to the farmer for feeding you?" Few people have ever had any special feeling of gratitude to the farmer. The very success of agriculture has made it uninteresting, or at least not a central issue to the rest of the culture. It is now being suggested that the very success of business—or, at least, of industry—may make it relatively uninteresting to the rest of the culture. Sometimes nothing fails like success.

Notes

1. The concepts of "surprise-free projection," "standard world," and related methodological tools are more fully explored by Anthony Wiener and myself in our book *The Year 2000* (New York: Macmillan, 1967).
2. The complete list may be found in Kahn and Bruce-Briggs, *Things to Come* (New York: Macmillan, 1972).
3. Nothing in recent discussions of "limits to growth" convinces me of the need to qualify this statement. While there may be some ultimate limits, they have not yet been identified or demonstrated.

TORGNY SEGERSTEDT, born in 1908, received his Ph.D. at the University of Lund in 1934 and served as Assistant Professor in Moral Philosophy at the same university 1934–38. In 1938 he became Professor of Moral Philosophy at Uppsala University and Professor of Sociology at the same university in 1947. He has been President of Uppsala University since 1955.

Torgny Segerstedt has been Chairman of the Social Science Research Council since 1959 and Chairman of the Bank of Sweden's Research Council since 1965. As Chairman of the University Committee, 1957–63, he played an important role in the reformation of the University organization.

He is the author of *The Nature of Social Reality* (1967) and has written many articles on philosophy, sociology, university-society relationships, and student unrest.

The Smaller Nation in the International Marketplace
TORGNY SEGERSTEDT

What will life be like for a small, highly industrialized country by the middle of the 1980s? My conjectures are based on a relatively uncertain assumption: the world will manage to avoid a third world war. I further assume that no state, big or small, will be able to have an isolated national existence. This applies especially to small nations. In 1985 Sweden will not be able to isolate herself in any area of life. Industry, trade, environment protection, research, leisure, and politics will be internationally oriented. Because of this, her national decisions, her autonomy and sovereignty will be undermined. This is, of course, an assumption or thesis that I must further develop and explain.

In my opinion, research and education are the factors which, more than anything else, will determine future development. This, of course, is a kind of dogma on my part, but it is based on observations of the tremendous role science and technology have played in development during the whole of the twentieth century. Of course, I may sometimes be doubtful as to whether this development can continue during the seventies and eighties at the same speed as it has done in the past.

155

Right now, one has a strong feeling that the great faith of the sixties in science and technology is decreasing. In any case, a considerable uncertainty is noticeable with regard to priorities. It is doubtful if space travel will be able to retain its great prestige value. But the moon shots attracted a great deal of money to research and kept scientists busy, who thereby contributed to the training of researchers. And even if you are doubtful about the importance of these moon shots, there still does not seem to be any alternative if money is to be found for research. A consequence of reduced funds, in a chain reaction that affects even the universities, is that many people employed in scientific fields are out of work.

On the other hand, a lot of problems are emerging —such as the problems of population, environment and resources, communication and mass media, education and urbanization—which can only be solved through continued, purposeful, single-minded research, which in its turn presupposes basic research. I do not think it is possible to reduce the speed of research other than temporarily, even though we may have to take into account a certain hostile attitude toward it, above all with regard to technical research, from certain youth groups. Even if this attitude is overcome, research presents many problems, not least with regard to costs. It seems as if research, especially applied research, is becoming continuously more costly. Basic research, too, demands ever-greater investments, which may make it difficult, maybe impossible, for small nations to keep up with the rapid advancement of the big nations.

I have found that the best way to appreciate the importance of science, and possible scientific breakthroughs, is to see them in relation to what I call the three basic functions of society: reproduction, socialization, and production. When I say that these three functions are basic I mean that every human group must (1) recruit new members in order to ensure its survival. This, in the final analysis, means biological reproduction. Furthermore (2) each group must bring up and educate its members, that is, make them part of society. And each group must (3) produce commodities to be able to protect itself against hunger, thirst, cold, and heat. Around these three basic functions one may observe different groups, such as the family, the school, the university, and the working groups. Communities may even be classified according to the way in which these groups are related. Thus, if one wants to look ahead, one can ask the following questions: what scientific breakthroughs can be expected during the next fifteen years; and how will these breakthroughs effect the different groups in relation to the basic functions?

It is evident that we can expect considerable scientific breakthroughs in the areas concerning the reproductive functions. We already know enough to separate the reproductive functions from sexual satisfaction. This in itself may mean a redesigning of the family. Already we have seen certain shifts in this direction, but perhaps the hippie communities and group sex are only fads or prototypes of a new social life. We have the means for family planning, but we have evidently also the knowledge to intervene more actively. Perhaps we may, in the near future, control the mixture of the races and genetic properties. I believe that our moral values will enable us to hold our ground against such intervention with natural reproduction. But one can never be too sure: we have already seen so many taboos collapse and the shifting of so many values, that we do not know what a purposeful, single-minded government may do in the future with such knowledge at its disposal. On the other hand, one must be careful not to dismiss these possibilities of manipulation as science fiction. Too many things which we thought impossible during the fifties have come true in the sixties. We can be sure that questions of reproduction or recruiting will be of ever-greater importance to Sweden in the seventies because she is going to feel the pressure of immigrants against her borders during the whole of the next two decades, while her own birth rate remains low. Surely, nobody believes that Sweden will be able to withstand the pressure which the world's growing population will exert.

I should think that the population question and the distribution of people will be *so* big an issue during the decades ahead of us that some kind of international institution will be created to try to solve it, an institution with considerable authority in relation to national governments. We speak of regulated immigration—even as regards students at our universities we meet this problem: there are hundreds of students from far-off universities and countries knocking at our doors.

In the future, the situation will probably be that Sweden will be allotted a certain quota of people of different categories to be absorbed every year and adjusted to her society. The Swedish age structure will, furthermore, be such that she will welcome young people to her country. The problem will be how to pay for such an immigration and adjustment. We can be sure that the absorption of immigrants into society will be costly. I do not think that, in the future, any country will be allowed to do what Switzerland now is thinking of doing—that is, expel a certain number of foreigners.* Great economic difficulties are expected in Switzerland if the plebiscite should reveal that the forces hostile to immigration are in a majority. We know that many Swedish industries and services would have to close if foreign labor was not available. With Switzerland as the first example of the consequences of inward-looking policies, one may ask if, in the future, independent national measures in this area can be allowed, or if it will be necessary to create international bodies with authority to distribute various population groups. It is my belief, therefore, that Sweden, Switzerland, and other countries who are considered relatively rich, will be enjoined to absorb a certain number of immigrants every year. It is already estimated that Sweden will annually receive about 20,000. This would increase her population to 9.25 million by the year 2000. I would guess that the estimated figure is far too low.

Whatever happens, immigration will put high demands on training and education. Sweden has already encountered these problems both with regard to youth and adult education; she must teach both children and adults the Swedish language. With regard to language, the children are evidently less of a problem. We have

---

* Sweden and Switzerland rely heavily upon immigrants from Finland and Southern Europe for unskilled and semi-skilled labor. In 1970, a proposed severe restriction on foreign labor was narrowly defeated in a Swiss plebiscite.—Ed.

already seen that the isolation of the adults presents greater problems. At the same time, the very fact that these immigrants come from another language area is an asset from which Sweden could benefit. Language is not the only problem in the adjustment process. There must also be an effort to bring the newcomers into the Swedish social system, into Swedish culture and Swedish political traditions. In this respect, Sweden cannot count on the same positive attitude as immigrants to Israel have revealed, for they feel that they have "come home" and, therefore, really want to be integrated. Sweden's aim must be to avoid the creation of underprivileged minorities—while these minorities may be demanding to keep their particular cultural characteristics, their religion, etc.

The immigrants present certain new or additional problems for Sweden's education system. The immigrants are, however, symptoms of international events which will influence her traditional educational outlook regardless of whether she is going to have any immigration problems or not. Sweden is already experiencing great uneasiness and a feeling of uncertainty within the educational field. The Swedish school system was planned for conditions on the labor market which no longer exist. Her school reformers of twenty or twenty-five years ago proceeded from what to them was a self-evident proposition, namely that education, to a great extent, should be a training for leisure. Most people, it was thought, would be occupied in soulless routine jobs. But these jobs would, on the other hand, take very little of their time. Therefore, people should be given opportunities which would allow them to spend their leisure time in a satisfying and worthwhile manner.

It is obvious that this vision was not altogether wrong. Our leisure time will most certainly increase. But we can, perhaps, say that Sweden started from an idea of a nationally limited leisure in the same way as she started from an idea of a nationally limited labor market with, to a large extent, traditional occupations. If one wants to discuss education, and especially education for the future, the questions seem to revolve around the future labor market and future occupations. One thing we know about the future labor market is that it is going to change rapidly; there will continuously be new types of occupations, with old occupations disappearing. It is estimated that about 30 per cent of today's occupations have been created since the Second World War.

Futurologists seem to agree that industrial production in the industrial countries will employ an ever-decreasing part of the national manpower. Bertil Olsson, Director-General of the Swedish National Labor Market Board, has mentioned 30 per cent as the probable figure for the future. My guess is that even this is too high. The share of agriculture will most certainly decrease still further, perhaps to 8 or 5 per cent. Sixty to 65 per cent, maybe 70 per cent, will be employed in different types of service occupations. This may mean that work in the future for large groups of people will not be as mechanical and monotonous as was believed twenty years ago when Sweden planned the new schools. Work may be more varied and demand more knowledge.

The brief indications may give some guidance to the future labor market. A general feature is the increasing tendency toward internationalization. We find it rather natural that many service industries should have an international outlook. We also find it natural that people occupied in the educational sector should be open to international views. We find it necessary for teachers on different levels to keep up with international debate.

But what will life be like for the people who will be occupied with the actual production, that is, those who will constitute the aforementioned 30 per cent of the total manpower? Looking at the development of the labor market during the sixties, one sees that within this sector also a shift has taken place toward more skilled labor, often toward work dependent on science. At the moment, it seems as if the labor shortage is primarily noticeable within the middle sector, that is, within the middle sector of qualified occupations. We are, however, witnessing a gradual stepping-up of the requirements. The jobs formerly done by unskilled labor are today performed by machines. This, however, seems to increase the demands for greater skills in the middle groups. Lumbering is an example. It was not long ago, actually only about a decade, that muscular strength was the important thing in forest work. Now this work is almost completely mechanized.

Swedish television recently showed a program about the social problems of low intelligence. Crane operators, for example, must now have mechanical knowledge and be quick on the uptake. This applies to more and more occupations. It certainly looks as if this movement toward higher requirements for jobs will continue. Here, too, one must reckon with internationalization, and this concerns not only industrial production and the social services, but also, to an equally high degree, the commercial service industry. But it also means that a big international problem in the future will be the care of people, that is, the care of those who, for one reason or another, cannot keep up with production, those who in the aforementioned TV program were called the "stupid ones." But there are also other handicapped groups, and we must in some way take care of them. It will be an important international question.

What does this internationalization mean in concrete terms? First and foremost, that the international outlook which has traditionally characterized Sweden's export industry will continue. This will create definite demands with regard to the education in languages, economy, and cultural anthropology of those who are going to work in this sector. But the important question for the small industrial countries will certainly be the relationship between the domestic and multinational industries. The decisive question is if the latter will become really international or merely the expression of industrial imperialism, which would mean that their real management will have its headquarters in one or the other of the big-power states and hence that the small countries will be unable to influence events. The future of the small industrial countries will, to a large extent, be dependent on how multinational companies develop. Dr. Drucker, in his fascinating book, *The Age of Discontinuity*, takes a rather optimistic view. He believes that the multinational companies will become really international both as regards structure and management and that management, therefore, will see the world as a single unit even when it comes to resources and environment. It is to be hoped that he will be proved right. What is to be feared, however, is a ruthless exploitation of the human and material resources of the small industrial countries, not to mention the developing countries. Dr. Drucker perhaps takes it too much for granted that top management is going to feel a continuously greater responsibility toward the communities in which they are active.

I have already pointed out that a decreasing part of Swedish manpower will be occupied in actual production. The same holds true for the labor market in the United States and no doubt also for the international labor market. On the other hand, both the social and commercial services—education, social care, mass media, and communications—are prerequisites for this production to function properly. This, in turn, puts high demands on the distribution of production profits. Those who consider themselves to be the actual producers must put up with being taxed for the benefit of the social and commercial services or certain parts thereof. It is my guess also that within this sector an international leveling out will take place, which may put the squeeze on a small country such as Sweden. Questions are already being asked in certain quarters about what will happen to Sweden's social benefits if she joins the Common Market and these same people warn against an internationalization of Swedish industry. Sweden will certainly have this problem of profit allocation during the seventies and eighties, even if she is allowed to live in isolation, though possibly on a smaller scale. Imagine an isolated Swedish labor market with 25 per cent in industrial production and 50 per cent in social-service occupations—the 25 per cent must somehow support the 50 per cent. On the other hand, it is certainly true that the 50 per cent, among which we find teachers, researchers, doctors, and social workers, in different ways help both the 25 per cent and the rest of the population to function. We have already seen how the education of immigrants is becoming an economic problem. It means that even if we look at it from a very limited national angle—and still more so if we see it from an international viewpoint—the 25 per cent who make the production wheels go round will have to feel a greater responsibility, or else they will have to be controlled in one way or the other so that they will be made to feel this responsibility. Herman Kahn has asked, "Who is actually thanking the farmers for producing all our food?" In the not-too-distant-future it will also be a question of "Who is thanking industry for producing all our commodities?" so that we, in different ways, can go on living.

This industrial output, and the minority which will produce it, must in the future be distributed over the whole population on both a national and international level. How this can be done in practice will, I think, be one of the big problems of the next twenty years.

Looking at the production function, we find a shift to service occupations due to new scientific breakthroughs. Everybody seems to agree on that, whether they are speaking of primary, secondary, tertiary, or quaternary occupations. We also find an increasing internationalization due particularly to a number of innovations based on scientific breakthroughs in communications and information, and we can be sure that Swedes and nationals of other small states will be employed by international companies, whether of a bureaucratic or industrial nature. It is also true that there is an increased dependence on science and, therefore, higher demands for knowledge in all occupations. There are new occupations with requirements for reeducation and retraining and also demands for a continuous renewal of knowledge. For a small country like Sweden there will surely be discussions in the future as to what type of production the aforementioned 25 per cent of the population shall be occupied with; whether the industries are going to specialize and, if so, what factors shall be decisive. We have already heard today that raw materials will not be the decisive factors that they were earlier.

I don't think that we will be able to live in isolation, and this will mean that the small nations will find it more and more difficult to determine for themselves the distribution of their wealth and their standard of living. I look upon this as a very grave problem indeed. The urbanized areas will expand and there is a risk that all over the world there will be growing slum areas populated with people who will have difficulties in keeping up with highly demanding competition due to insufficiencies in their intellectual or emotional equipment. Clear signs of the emergence of such a group can already be seen in the United States and is discernible even in Sweden. We can also see how people voluntarily place themselves outside the demands of modern society—the hippie movement is an expression of this. But both the voluntary and involuntary groups represent distribution problems which we must solve.

Perhaps, in the future, other factors will strengthen international responsibility. Let us hope so. One such factor could be the big efforts we now have to make in order that our natural resources shall be sufficient.

Both Daniel Bell and Peter Drucker stress the fundamental importance of theoretical knowledge for modern society. "Knowledge has become the central economic resource," says Dr. Drucker in his *The Age of Discontinuity.* The knowledge he is speaking of, however, is not knowledge acquired once and for all, but knowledge that must continually be renewed and adjusted in accordance with the latest research results. It is very difficult to predict the occupational panorama of the future, but this much is sure: that man must always be prepared for occupational changes, and he must, therefore, continuously educate himself or be educated. This education may be done within the companies or outside, but it is crucial.

The changes I have already indicated with regard to new citizens—in Sweden only about 75 per cent will be added through biological reproduction, the rest will come through immigration—will, considering the continuous shifts on the labor market, put high demands on her educational system. As already pointed out, Sweden must be able to integrate the immigrants into her social system and that needs highly qualified teachers. This integration must be carried out without creating too-disruptive generation gaps between the immigrants and their children. The problems of the immigrants can be clearly seen, but, of course, the same problems exist with regard to the native Swedish population. Occupation patterns will change and the demands for adjustment will also be felt by Swedes themselves. This means reeducation and further training. If not, there will be big generation gaps in the Swedish population, which means that very soon many people will not be able to hold their own on the labor market. The awareness of this lies behind today's drive for adult education.

The development I have outlined puts many other

demands on the education system. A basic point has been the increased internationalization of the labor market. A good illustration of this trend is the recent battle for power within the Billman company. When Minister Wickman was in the United States a few months ago, he said that he welcomed the flow of American capital to Sweden (annual investments now amount to about 350 million Swedish crowns).* This internationalization is still more natural within research, education and a number of other spheres. The education industries will certainly be internationally oriented. Consequently we in Sweden must in every way try to keep up with international scientific debate. Research is, however, as I have already said, becoming continuously more costly, both as regards operation costs and investments.

I believe, therefore, that the role and task of a small country may be to conduct basic research, because it is the least costly role. Our work is innovation. If we are unable to assert ourselves in this field, we may not be able to play any role at all, but in our scientific work we may make ourselves indispensable by being pioneers within certain sectors of basic research. We should back the most brilliant minds in basic research, both our own and internationally acknowledged scientists. At the same time, we must bear in mind that a prerequisite for the successful work of these talented people is a high standard in the research team and the staff who surround them, and Sweden must bear this in mind in her educational policy.

Another important point for future research is the

*Five Swedish crowns = one U.S. dollar (1970).—Ed.

total view, not the least important if you want to avoid a negative attitude to research. A large part of the world's misery can be said to lie in the fact that nobody tries to see the totality and the interaction between the different fields of research.

One may discuss the effects of research projects on (1) the biosphere, (2) society, and (3) the individual. It is important to keep these three aspects together. Changes in the biosphere affect the individual and society, but at the same time, changes in society affect the individual and the biosphere. We must strive to develop a system to measure and evaluate these reactions. We must also try to achieve that total view which makes possible a discussion of priorities for different scientific areas. Here, too, small nations may be able to play a role, because they can present alternatives. They can do this because they do not themselves have to choose; they can instead create and submit different courses of action.

A small country can never decide on priorities; this must always be up to the big nations. As a result, a small country must always endeavor to educate people who, through their proficiency, can assert themselves on the international labor market, in international research and in different international bodies. Sweden will attract the attention of multinational businesses or organizations only through a high standard of competence. Just as in science, the demand for talent and high standards must apply throughout a company's structure; the middle jobs are also going to require more and more knowledge.

OTA SIK, born in Plzen, Czechoslovakia, in 1919, graduated from the School of Political and Social Sciences in Prague in 1952, and became Professor of Economics in 1957. Between 1961 and 1968 he was Head of the Economic Institute of the Academy of Sciences in Prague.

Between 1963 and 1968 Ota Sik was Chairman of the Government Commission for the reform of the Czechoslovakian economy, and from April 1968 to August 1968 was Deputy Prime Minister. Ota Sik was a member of the Czech Communist Party, 1940–69, and member of the Central Committee, 1958–69. He was granted political asylum in Switzerland in 1970 and is presently Professor of Economics at the University of Basel. Among his books are *Plan and Market Under Socialism* (1967) and *Facts About the Czechoslovakian Economy* (1968).

He was granted political asylum in Switzerland in 1970 and is presently Professor of Economics at the University of St. Gallen. Among his books are *Plan and Market Under Socialism* (1967), *Czechoslovakia—The Bureaucratic Economy* (1968), and *The Third Way* (1972).

Plan and Market
in Socialism— A European Model
for the Eighties
OTA SIK
(translated from the German by Gabrielle M. David)

A socialist synthesis of planning and marketing may be the economic model of the future. Combined with a scientifically and democratically organized political system, it is the social picture of the future which may be called a humane society.

Let me make a few introductory remarks: I have arrived at this picture of the future on the basis of analyses of the current so-called socialist (Eastern) society, as well as of capitalist (Western) society. I believe, that within both societies certain growing contradictions exist, the solution to which may well lead to the creation of a new social framework, which could mean not only overcoming both these current systems but, at the same time, could become a unifying factor for society. Even though I, of course, continue to be convinced that national states will not yet disappear and that every country will maintain its historically imposed form of society, I believe however, that certain general basic human principles may prevail.

That is why current blatant contradictions in the system may disappear and the states may well come closer to one another. This may also promote certain steps toward confederation aimed at eliminating violent actions and warlike resolutions of possible differences between states.

Development toward this unifying humanization is, however, a very difficult process. It will not occur automatically and it will not succeed without political vindication of the reactionary, power-hungry, and warlike forces of extremism which exist within both systems. Even though reactionary forces still exist, bound by their interests, which are based mainly on primitive emotions and who tend toward demagogy in both systems I am convinced that reason and the interests of progressive and humane groups of society will win in the end. Otherwise the world would be destroyed by atomic war.

I thus hold an optimistic point of view toward the resolution of the existing contradictions and would like to present them somewhat more clearly. What are the contradictions which lead to the model of a socialist plan and market economy?

Let us first look at the reasons which lead to a socialization as well as at the nature of this socialization; and then look at the one which will bring about an economic planning and which form it will assume; and finally look at those which will affect the specific market relations.

By socialization, I mean the vindication of contradictions between two groups of human beings, one of which has a predominate interest in developing capital while the other one is mainly interested in increasing its salary and social security. The former Marxist definition of the contradictions between capital and labor says little about current contradictions within production and simplifies the social problems. I will, therefore, characterize the contradiction within production more explicitly. The reflection of this contradiction in society can be seen in the interests of man, in the contradictions between interests of different classes in society, some of which are interested in the growth of capital while others are explicitly uninterested in this development and have a definite interest in salary.

To describe the first group as capitalists would be an oversimplification. Besides real capitalists (i.e. private entrepreneurs, large shareholders, bankers, land owners, etc.), managers and heads of large companies and concerns (whether or not they themselves are already capitalists), economic ministers, and other civil servants of higher ranks responsible for economic development also belong to this group. Today these social classes are the only ones concerned with and responsible for the development of capital.

The optimum development of capital—and I am thinking here of capital in the form of the means of production—the steady growth, modernization, the most effective use of capital, are the foundation of every social development. Without this effective development, no humanization of society, no decrease in working hours, no high-level cultural development can exist. This development of production funds is, however, not merely a matter of technical and economic knowledge but also of certain economic interests. Bound by their interests, it was the capitalists' historical progressive role to develop capital. This fact was also pointed out by Marx. But because of their position they had to continuously enlarge private capital at the expense of the workers, of their competitors, and of society as a whole. The concern with capital accumulation in the past was basically accompanied by a lack of knowledge of the total economic interrelationships of society.

With the growing power of the large concerns and corporations, the capitalist private interest was no longer sufficient to secure the necessary development of capital. Alongside the real capitalists appeared the modern managers with their gigantic apparatus, increasingly taking their place in decision making. Propelled as much by their own interest in maintaining their position as managers of a successful company as by their concern for the capitalists' profits, they used more and more modern economic knowledge and scientific methods to secure and increase the growth of capital.

Current development is, moreover, specifically characterized by the increasingly larger and more important role of the state in securing a balanced and steady growth of capital in a balanced economy. Along with this function of the state, new groups of civil servants inevitably arise whose interests are linked with the long-range optimal development of capital in the social scale. In influencing capital development, they rely to a great extent on the state apparatus.

No matter how important society's concern to increase capital and no matter how important all economic knowledge is in trying to secure an optimal economic development, the lack of interest of the broad masses of the population in capital accumulation will become an increasingly difficult obstacle to its growth.

The great masses of producers, who possess no capital and are also excluded from any decision making in its development, are hostile to capital, have no interest in its effective exploitation, are even emotionally against its growth, and are only concerned about increasing salaries. This currently leads to a slowing down of development. Under current conditions of highly concentrated production, because of the decrease of the capitalists' direct influence on production, the inevitable compromising role of the manager vis-à-vis full employment, the even more unstable position of the civil servants who are subject to twofold political pressure, and the growing discoveries of new possibilities for production and effectiveness in the huge concerns will create a noticeable break in development for these antagonistic interests.

At the current level of development of the forces of production, the enormous concentration of capital and production and the fateful decisions to be made for the development of corporations become increasingly important to thousands and thousands of employees. It is unreasonable to continue to see these employees in the role of alienated anticapitalists. It is unclear why the interests of only small groups of people should be connected with the development of capital while the large masses of producers do not consider this interest in capital as theirs.

To create an interest in capital among all working people would at the same time create a congruence between their conscious short-range salary interests and their rising consciousness of long-range work and salary interests (conditioned by capital development). The generating of an interest in the development of capital would be the creation of consistent short- and long-range interests among working people. The creation of such interest is, however, not to be compared with the attainment of considerable knowledge for optimizing this development. As well, the capitalists (the owners of capital) who are interested in the development of capital today, no longer need to possess the required knowledge for the optimum development of capital. This is the business of the managers, of whom nowadays specific capabilities, knowledge and experience in order to optimize capital development are required. They could, however, more easily fulfill their tasks *with* the existing capital interests of the producers than against their interests.

According to current official dogmatic Marxist theory, such an interest by the producers is to be created through the nationalization of companies. In reality, Soviet nationalization of companies signifies such a strong bureaucratization of their management that it not only fails to create an interest for the workers in the development of capital, but on the contrary, the companies' concerns become even more alienated to them than before. They continue to have no participation in management, have no direct share in the results, have no influence on the development of capital, and are not interested in it. Because of centrally planned salary funds they often fail to have sufficient interest in unlimited increase in work productivity. Monotonously phrased propaganda, formal competitive organizations, and so-called workers committees for the improvement of production cannot create an economic interest in the effective exploitation of the means of production.

Thus in so-called "socialist" society, the only real economic interest of the workers is in their salaries and bonuses, while the development of capital is left completely to the party and state officials, particularly to the planning bureaucracy. Since, however, their interest is not really an economic interest in the development of capital, but is basically only an interest in power, and since this power interest is satisfied with a one-sided, purely quantitative, ineffective, uneconomic, and antioptimal development of production, the earlier interest in capital is eliminated but not replaced by a new one. What are the consequences? A steady decrease in the efficiency of investment, an average obsolescence of the means of production, of machines, a lag in technical development in comparison with the West and, as a result, an increasingly slower rate of growth of the national per capita income of the population and its standard of living— these are the consequences.

The solution to the contradiction between the necessity for an optimal development of capital and the disinterest of the broad mass of producers in such a development in industrially developed countries, (in capitalist as well as bureaucratic socialist countries) can, in my opinion, be sought only in the creation of a really direct interest by the producers in the development of capital through democratic socialization.

All workers in a company should become the coowners and, in this sense, should participate directly in the capital stocks. Only when every working member of the company obtains, beyond his working salary, a share of the capital which will guarantee him a corresponding share in the profits can there be a rise in economic interest among the workers in the effective exploitation and expansion of capital funds. It is however necessary that all co-workers not only obtain a corresponding claim—

ie., a certificate for a share in the value of the existing capital which is invested in the company—but also of every increase in capital expansion (growth investment) which will give them a right to future profits. Capital growth should then consist mainly of profit sharing, for example, 70 or 80 per cent (this would have to be calculated precisely) of the profit sharing of the co-workers would be paid out in certificates and only, let us say, 30 or 20 per cent in cash for immediate use. This would guarantee that the greater part of the co-worker's profit sharing would again be used to increase capital, and at the same time create an interest in the development of capital among the co-workers. The distribution of the capital stock of the existing capital could then be divided up in different ways—for example, according to the length of time employed in the company, etc.

These so-formed capital growth funds (investment funds) can, according to entrepreneurial considerations, either be invested in the company or used to form a new company and invested in the bank. Every arrangement outside of the company must be decided upon by the company's board of directors. The capital investment to form a completely new company (so far as it isn't a smaller enterprise within the existing company) cannot be regarded as the procurement of new property for the old company. The new company will in turn be regarded as independent property of the newly-formed collective and the capital invested in its formation will be considered to be long-term credit, which, with relatively high interest rates (higher than the founding company would get for its capital in the bank), would be paid back to the founding company.

The capital of a collective company, which gradually will become for the most part collective property (expressed in certificates), should not become centralized (bureaucratized). The co-workers (and co-owners) must continuously be informed of the use made of the capital and of expected profit-sharing developments, and they should have an influence on the company's board of directors (council) over these developments. The certificates cannot be sold, and if a co-worker moves to another company, they should be sold back to the company, at a stipulated price (for example, half of the nominal worth). At the death of a co-worker, the certificates would be automatically returned to the company (without compensation in case of eventual inheritance). The retirement of a co-worker would end his claim to further certificates, but until his death he could continue to have a claim on the portion of the share of profits which should be coming to him according to his certificates (20% or 30%).

The main concerns in the creation of capital-sharing are socialization of interest and responsibility for capital development. Today I consider these to be much more current and important problems in the development of work productivity than the largely obsolete theories of socialization. These lead continually to governmental alienation from the means of production and to the bureaucratization of development. Besides the socialization of capital responsibility there is the limiting of excessive wealth in the hands of single persons, which creates social imbalance and gives someone the possibility of having greater political influence than the ordinary person would have.

Starting from both these aspects, the formation of capital-sharing and a position on stock ownership in western countries can be established. From the point of view of the development of work productivity, the complete elimination of stock ownership would be very questionable, since stockholding is now as much as ever an important function of allocation. As soon as general capital-sharing is brought into being and all working persons can take part according to the length of time they have worked, the privilege of owning private capital and its class reaction will disappear and the only problem remaining will be the limitation of stock capital accumulated through generations. States which have a democratic political system and which carry out a program of capital-sharing and the limitation of stock ownership have, besides taxes (progressive inheritance tax, income tax, etc.), the possibility of legally stipulating the maximum share of the profit which can be used to pay dividends.

Capital stock sharing is the economic basis for the socialization of the interest in capital as well as the basis for socialization of the responsibility for the development of capital. This process must then be accordingly completed by the election of a company head (company advisory council) elected from among the co-workers (co-owners). The council would decide on economic policy, on the company's principles for development, the statutes, and the major questions of integration and disintegration, etc. The council should not replace management, but should review the long-range activities of management. This advisory council has thus the right to remove or appoint the directors. These chosen advisers must be specifically interested in the long-range developments of the capital stock, for example, through special shares in profit growth for, let us say five years, to keep the members of this advisory council really interested in the long-range effective development of the company. The council itself will in the long run be controlled by the worker's assembly (ownership assembly). All concrete (short- and long-range) production and investment decisions are the concern of management, insofar as these correspond to the principal goals of the company advisory council.

A democratic socialization of this nature can bridge the contradiction between owners and nonowners, between capital interests and salary interests, between bureaucratic management and productive labor, between the long- and short-range interest of the workers, and can achieve a more effective exploitation of development of capital funds. That is why this will be achieved sooner or later in the East as well as in the West. The concrete methods, forms, and duration of these processes will differ in different systems and countries. The duration will depend especially on how quickly the progressive groups in society, conscious of the necessity for socializing the capital interest, can assert themselves politically against the conservative capital and power forces. This answers the first contradiction, the solution to which I see in a modern democratic socialization. I will now turn to the problem of planning.

When I speak of political economic planning, I mean a specific goal structure for a macroeconomic development through the state, which would correspond to the interests of the majority of the working population and would be set above the goals of the individual companies. These macroeconomic goals should not run against a long-range optimal economic development and should be carried out by engaging the means that are actually capable to secure the realization of those goals. In planning, we are concerned with trying to obviate the contradictions between the goals of individual concerns and the democratically attained goals of society, perhaps even solving them in time. As is well known today, the pursuit of goals in the individual companies through completely self-sufficient, spontaneous development leads to a national economic development which does not always correspond to the interests and goals of the majority of the working population. That is why in Western states the idea has been increasingly accepted that economic development should be influenced by the state, using financial and other economic instruments, so that certain goals can be obtained which correspond to the interests of the majority (full employment, monetary stability, growth, balance of payments, etc.).

However, we are concerned here with more or less lasting goals, which a balanced growth aspires to, but during which fundamental changes in the distribution of national income, in social structure, in the type of consumption, etc., are usually not pursued. Under such a system production and the market are developed spontaneously, and do not always correspond to the long-range interests of the population (for example, by unnecessary production through the manipulation of the market, or by exaggerating the changes resulting from fashion in demand, etc.,) or completely one-sided materialistic consumer goals are pursued with complete disregard of public needs in extension of leisure time, in higher cultural development, in more rapidly increasing the educational level, etc. Unfortunately, war and armament goals also lead to one-sided productivity which can always find a market. In short, it is a development of productivity, in which the latter becomes an end in itself, men continue to become alienated, and the humanizing of society is not even considered.

In order to achieve a humanization of society, it is not sufficient to pursue the currently fashionable goals of growth and balance with countercyclical policies, but besides these goals, it is necessary to create other significant changes in the development of production, distribution, and consumption which should be pursued according to the interests of the majority of the population.

But in order to set up these goals in a realistic way one must calculate the fundamental macroeconomic relationships, in advance, which means to work out the plans. To give society a really democratic choice for its future development it is necessary to work out several different plans with a declaration not only of alternative goals, but also of different means for their attainment, including pointing out all potentially unpopular steps which may be expected in the pursuit of certain goals. Only on the basis of this kind of macroeconomic alternative planning do the representative popular organizations have a democratic freedom of choice and the people a possibility of determining their own future.

Even though the notion of political economic planning was discovered by Marx, planning assumed shape in bureaucratic socialism, in which neither the people nor the political organizations have any real freedom of choice. Planning follows a totally simplistic goal, that of the quickest possible growth of a centrally required production. At the same time this central planning provides —for dogmatic ideological reasons—for the elimination of the market and is therefore unable to rely on market price, market criteria, and market incentives. Therefore, the development of production can only be carried forward by a directive plan in quantitative natural values.

However, a central organization cannot plan in detail the entire production of some millions of concrete types of products. Even with the aid of an entire computer system (currently seen as the most modern equipment for planning in the Soviet Union) it is impossible to set up such a detailed and concrete plan. That is why planning in the socialist states must be calculated in terms of aggregates. These aggregates are expressed through totally administrative prices, corresponding neither to cost nor to the market. Prices are supposed to be relatively stable and serve only for calculating the number of products planned.

Without economic prices, however, the calculating of efficiency and that of substitution possibilities are quite impossible. In short, the actual economic problems get lost. Besides, there is no practical possibility of working out alternative plans and comparing them to one another from the standpoint of efficiency. The plan can only be engineered with the aid of input-output data (in physical units) obtained from the companies, and inevitably includes enormous and uncontrollable reserves. On the basis of those one-sided data from the companies the plan is sewn together with the aid of central empirical planning informations. It firmly fixes production which— even though it has been formally balanced with the existing demand—can neither raise any new and progressive demands nor can it get flexibly adapted to the changes in the given demand. On the contrary, this is—as far as its quality, technology and costs are concerned—the increasingly conservative production lagging more and more behind the development of the capitalist production. The equilibrium of input and output is also balanced in global aggregated quantities, while the process of disaggregating of those quantities within the companies leads to increasingly growing contradictions between production and consumption.

This type of planning cannot be maintained in the long run because it makes a socialist economy incapable of competing with capitalist development. If socialism is to survive at all, it must make a transition from bureaucratic directive planning to a democratic macroeconomic orientation planning. In a socialist society, the main concern in the future will also be the creation of humane goals of development for society, and the corresponding macroeconomic calculations. On the basis of economic prices, the most effective possible developments will be calculated and out of a few different variants the plan will be chosen in a democratic way. This plan will not set up any binding quantitative production figures for the companies, but the government will try to achieve the development that has been planned by employing the indirect means, such as financial instruments, tax policy, credit policy, foreign-trade policy, monetary policy, etc.

The gradual development of such ways of planning

in the West and future transition to it in the East would mean the disappearance of further antagonisms in the systems of today. Whereas obstacles to this development of planning in the West are relatively minor, in the Eastern countries prevail the dogmatic ideological prejudices of avowedly bureaucratic interests (enormous planning and managerial apparatus) which see in every departure from state planning the undermining of their existence. They will try to frustrate any attempt to eliminate central company regulation and thwart the striving for individual corporate independence. For the same reasons, they fight strongly against the notion of the necessity of a market in socialism and call it an antisocialist theory. Let me proceed to the problem of the market.

The market with its relative autonomy is self-evident in capitalism. It seems superfluous here to explain its necessity. Of course, it is an incomplete market with unequal conditions for the participants and oligarchical and monopolistic drawbacks. Nevertheless, this market forces production to respect the concrete demands of the consumers. Regardless of how these demands arose, (more or less they are always due to production) they are relatively independent from production through the possibility of choice by the consumers. This is a built-in factor of the market. This freedom of choice also forces the producers, above their own economic interests in increasing income to further the development of productive forces, increase in productivity and effectiveness of the production mechanisms, qualitative development, and flexibility of structural development. All this coincides with the interests of people as consumers.

This positive economic function of the market is

often disguised by the contradictions which show up on the market, but are not caused by it. Production is always only familiar with the current market, but never exactly knows the market of the future. Changes in production itself (new products, changes in structure and cost, etc.), as well as changes in the distribution of national income (salaries, profits, taxes, etc.), bring about changes in supply and demand which cannot be predicted precisely by the individual companies. Nevertheless, they are forced to make in advance decisions (often a long time in advance) upon production, especially upon investment for the future market.

That is why in the past, production always was in major contradiction with the resulting market. Large surpluses were produced; other products were in insufficient amount; certain companies went bankrupt; others made enormous profits; periodic crises were then unavoidable. Marxist theory described this development as a spontaneous, anarchical development and saw its cause simply in the existence of private ownership and in the market itself. With elimination of the market, anarchy was supposed to disappear as well. Through state planning of production and through the nationalization of the means of production, production was supposed to be brought precisely and directly in accord with demand.

According to this simplistic theory, not only private ownership of the means of production was eliminated in the socialist states, but also the market was limited to such extent that its most important economic functions disappeared. Nevertheless it was not possible to bring production in accord with demand but, on the contrary, the contradiction between production and consumption was even greater than in present-day capitalism. A one-sided assault on consumption by production occurred; moreover, the impetus to effectiveness, productivity, qualitative development and flexibility of the structure of production disappeared.

It became clear that the market can not be replaced by a centrally directed planning because no central organ in a highly developed industrial economy can plan in detail the production of millions of types of products in all its ramifications. Nor can it foresee future demand in detail. Plans remain, as we have seen, global aggregate plans, while in the companies their disaggregation and transformation into the concrete and detailed production decisions are free from any pressure from competition, from market incentives (income is no longer tied to market results), from market price signals, and even from the necessity to give consideration to demand (global achievement of plans suffices, without any consideration as to whether the goods correspond to demand or whether selling is forced by a shortage of goods or whether production is piling up in warehouses or whether they are being dumped on easy foreign markets or if finally, after a longer period of time, they will wind up as unused products, etc.).

Under these conditions the completely one-sided domination of the producers over the consumers came about, together with the easiest conditions of production for them (without the necessity of qualitatively improving production) and the most complete monopolizing of production. Instead of overcoming anarchy in production, instead of planning production in accordance with social demands, anarchy increased and so complete a disregard of these demands occurred, as had never been possible before.

This is the confirmation that it is not the market which brings about the contradiction between production and consumption but, on the contrary, it adds to the harmonization of production and consumption. Rising contradictions and connected losses are the result: (1) of the impossibility of predicting the detailed development of the market and all the factors which influence it, and (2) of the objectively existing contradiction between the interests of people as producers and their interests as consumers, whereby without the market and competition, the one-sided interests of producers (in socialist companies as well) are always the decisive ones in decision making for production and are carried through at the cost of the consumer's interests.

Through competition, although it might be only potential competition, and through the market incomes the producers are forced to respect the needs of the consumers, since higher incomes would and could be obtained as a result of improvements in production, more advanced technology, more adequate structure of output and lower costs of production, in comparision with the competitors. As soon as the pressure of the market and competition begins to show signs of weakening and the big producers are given the possibility of manipulating the market and the freedom of choice of the consumers is limited, the one-sided interests of the producers begin to manifest themselves at the cost of the consumers. That is why the elimination of competition and of the market pressure always means for the producers the facilitating of their future developments, but always at the cost of potentially effective and qualitative developments. These tendencies already exist within capitalism and grow especially with the large companies, conglomerates, and monopolies but can only gain complete superiority through absolute monopolization and liquidation of the market under bureaucratic socialism.

That is why dogmatic Marxist theories, and some theories developed in the West as well, which try to minimize the role of the market, are in fact one-sided producer theories. They disregard the interests of people as consumers and completely neglect the necessary humanization of human society, which cannot be achieved through the one-sided domination of producers.

No matter how progressive the theories concerned with the planning as a substitute of the market and those of the subjection of the market to planned production seem to be, they are in reality regressive because they ignore the fact that every development of production is not *just* a matter of knowledge but also a matter of interest. Since the objective interests of the producer cannot be removed and the objective knowledge of detailed concrete production through a central organization cannot be optimally secured, the elimination of the market leads to a completely one-sided, even arbitrary decision making by producers. No non-economic moral, political or ideological influence can eliminate the objective existence of the antagonism between the interests of the producers and those of the consumers at the current level of development of the forces of production.

Planning cannot replace the market, it can only complement it. Since the market of the present is always a criterion of the past production, but never can determine future decisions on production—in other words, has little say in its own future development—planning should try to help and give shape to the future market. We are not just speaking of the knowledge of future market development, but at the same time about the desired influence of its development.

In our plans we should not only fix the knowledge of the future market based on the market's development in the past, but we must try to model the changes of this market based on the present desires of the society. To achieve a reliable knowledge of the future market the central planning organ needs a further development and improvement of the methods and ways in which the large companies and corporations can predict the development of future market. The state, naturally, has much more complete information and today possesses definite analytical methods and models with which it can predict the future rough outline of market developments and of certain existing developments in production and distribution. Here too, only aggregates can be used and only macroeconomic equations can be calculated. This knowledge may be of great help to future decision making of companies and especially for their investments. But the moment one tries to impute macro values to the companies in order to bind them to macro values and production goals, it becomes necessary to make the transition from approximately known and predictable macro processes to detailed decisions. It would mean to violate the companies and deprive them of their flexible reacting to the market. It is only the industrial managements who can make decisions on detailed production or on concrete market development.

How can one influence the future market? The development of the market may be influenced in its macrostructure and in its rate of growth. Primarily through intervention in income distribution, through tax policy, national budgetary policy, credit policy, etc., considerable changes in the development of the market can be achieved. But the manipulation of the market must not be performed according to the one-sided interests of the producers. It must be accomplished through democratically obtained changes in development, as I have said previously, through a choice made from alternative plans using democratic methods, through the confrontation of different interests—producer and consumer interests. Even here, during the months of the Prague Spring,* we considered a parliament consisting of a producers' house and a consumers' house to guard the humane development interests of the people in every sense, not just material consumption but also cultural development, educational development, and, in general, the life style and the pursuit of social, progressive development goals.

For example, a planned decrease in one-sided market-oriented production in favor of a planned expansion of education, health services, scientific and cultural development, etc., would of course influence the market as well. This influence on the market must be considered in the macroeconomic plan and it serves as an important piece of information for the decision making of the companies in the future.

This type of a democratically influenced, macro-

*Spring 1968, before the Soviet Army terminated the experiments of Dr. Sik and his colleagues.—Ed.

economically regulated development of the market which maintains its fundamental functions and is further promoted by the goal-consciousness of the state's antimonopolistic policy is, in my opinion, a progressive step. It corresponds as well to the existing possibility for the attainment of scientifically grounded economic knowledge by the state as well as to the respect for objectively conditioned contradictions between producer and consumer interests. It leads to the objectivity of planning and concrete production decisions by confrontation of different interests and the playing off of one against the other; it does not lead to subjective decision making by suppressing the interests of the social majority by the one-sided interests of the powerful producers or by a small group of power bureaucrats. That is why such a development of the market will, sooner or later, occur in the socialist countries as well.

A society where the contradictions between capital and salary interests, between companies and social interests, and between producers and consumers interests are to be solved through a socialist plan and market economy will not only obtain a more efficient development of the productive forces, but will primarily subordinate the economic development to humane social goals. It will be the beginning of overcoming the current alienation of human beings. The labor divisions in society will not yet be entirely alleviated, but the alienation of human beings from their own means of production will disappear. Human beings will be able to see, to a much greater extent, microeconomic as well as macroeconomic decision making, and as a result the contradictions between leaders and followers will decrease or even disappear. The one-sided materialistic consumer interests will be expanded through increasingly stronger cultural, scientific, and generally human interests, and on the basis of effective production and an increase in leisure time a considerable enrichment of human interests and relationships will be brought about.

This humane economic development is unthinkable without a more thorough democratization of society and the overcoming of all totalitarian forms of government. Only through the elimination of such political systems, in which monopolistic power groups suppress all progressive and new ideas, can a really modern democratic socialist development be achieved. That is why the necessary transition to a socialist planned-market economy will mean a difficult political struggle in bureaucratic socialist countries. The power bureaucracy, among other ways, maintains its power through the manipulation of people, by placing them in office and by removing them from office (through a so-called cadre policy). It stands in opposition to any democratic tendencies of development, any attempts toward autonomy by companies, and anything that can lead to the independence of people from their manipulators.

In the West as well as in the East, there are strong opponents to such a reform tendency, who fear that this development will take away their social privileges, their position of superiority, and their positions of power. Throughout history conservative forces have existed, whose conservatism was derived from economic and power interests which they have always hidden behind ideological arguments. These forces always find willing ideologists who are prepared to vilify everything new and reforming as a "heresy, unreality, naïveness."

In the West are strong forces who cannot stand any socialist ideas and in the East are those who will not consider any democratization. In both places these conservative forces are adamant defenders of the current system and seem to be unreconcileable opponents. However one should not exaggerate these seeming differences too much. Some are always prepared to maintain their position by thoroughly undemocratic methods while others, out of fear of democratization, are prepared to bureaucratize the system even more and to deprive socialism of the last remaining bits of its illusory splendor.

One should not forget the possibility of a reactionary convergence of undemocratic, one-sided production and power interests, hiding behind a bureaucratic, fascistic and antihumanist development of the current systems. These forces which stand behind such a tendency are not concerned with achieving a better system, but only with their own narrow interests. They see themselves threatened and would be prepared to throw mankind into a dreadful war.

I am convinced, however, that the humanist, socialist democratic ideas and forces will be victorious in the end. Progressive economic development cannot be halted. In the West, especially in the Western European countries as well as in the Eastern European countries (even if incomparably more difficult because of the lack of freedom of ideas and information) consciousness is being raised by the contradictions and obstacles which are slowing down a more effective and humane social development. Intelligentsia are always the first carriers and proponents of new ideas. Among the workers in the socialist countries, new ideas tend to ripen more slowly, but once a breakthrough occurs, as in Czechoslovakia, it cannot be pushed back by a dogmatic, racist, and stultifying ideology. The current reactionary trends in these countries are merely a sign of the increasingly stronger progressive forces which in the long run cannot be suppressed.

The Czech ideas and events were only the beginning. They have brought about a complex new social picture. To many timely questions, Czechoslovakia has given a great number of new answers. Despite the forceful suppression of the Czech experiment its theoretical foundations are more alive in Europe today than ever before. The process of this development of ideas cannot be stopped. Within ten to fifteen years, it may take on a progressive, practical reality in one country or another because the time is almost ripe for a changeover to a new political power and to make a political force from an idea.

The model of the democratic humane socialist society can be considered the model of the European political future whose beginning could lie in the 1980s. Furthermore, it will bring together human beings in the entire world and will finally be victorious against bureaucratic forces, against the extreme warmongers, against the nationalist and racist rousing of people, and against narrow-minded power interests.

The Future of the Corporation
HERMAN KAHN

The conference clarified and elaborated themes that most of the participants have been exploring for many years. To take me, for an example, while the focus of my policy research studies since about 1950 was mostly on technological, social, political, national security, arms control, and developmental-type issues, I, of course, had to take some interest in business issues as well. However, as a result of the Malmo conference my interest in business issues by greatly aroused and deepened. I have since then concluded that one major concept (advanced mainly by Drucker and Burnham)—that the impact of business would be one of the most interesting things going on in the second half of the twentieth century, particularly in connection with what we now call at Hudson "the superindustrial culture"—is absolutely correct. Further, the particular aspect of business that became the most interesting is probably the role of transnational corporation.

But actually, with the above partial exception, this conference mostly focused attention on what Bell and others (including Hudson) have called the "post-industrial culture." But I now believe that it is important to note that this post-industrial culture that emerges around the year 2000 in the developed part of the world, will be preceded and accompanied by the super-industrial culture. Thus, there are about 250 million cars in the world today. While there is a revolt by intellectuals against cars emerging in North America, Western Europe, and Japan, the world is still just entering the age of the automobile. I would guess there will be almost a billion cars in the world in the year 2000. Today the world uses about fifteen billion barrels of oil per year, and there is much talk of impending shortages. Nevertheless, I would argue that if all these cars are powered by internal combustion engines,* then by the year 2000 we will be using about fifty to a hundred billion barrels of liquid (or liquefied) fossil fuels.

Today the world annually produces about three-quarter billion tons of steel. Again it seems to me to be a reasonable conjecture that the end of the century will see two or three billion tons of steel per year produced despite much talk in recent years of overproduction. In other words, while we often think of the industrialization process as being in some ways passé, most of the industrialization of the world still has to be done. Similarly, while many in the developed world are increasingly conscious of the problems of pollution, difficulties of keeping up with change generally, and the desirability of limiting economic growth, we are likely soon to be swamped by growth, technological changes, and related

---

*Recent design breakthroughs (Wankel, stratified charge, supplemented hydrogen fueling, etc.) make a trivial-emission internal combustion engine probable.

issues. Then looking back from the twenty-first century, today is likely to be seen simply as a beginning rather than a mature and fulfilled process. Of course, many people disagree with this perspective; in fact they make almost the exact opposite point. They liken our current situation to that of a young man who has inherited a great fortune and is living high off the hog for the time being and rampantly running through his inheritance. However, double-entry bookkeeping will soon catch up with him. These people deny that we are emerging to a permanently higher plateau of consumption and material quality of life, characterized by the term "post-industrial culture," but rather see today as a kind of a golden age that will never be reproduced. We will not in this book deal much with the quarrel between these two schools of thought—between the neo-Malthusian and the post-industrial culture perspectives.

However, it is important to decide which of these two views is correct before one can get any sense on how to judge the discussion in this volume. Unfortunately we will not have the space to do so here. Let me simply assert that Hudson is currently engaged in a major study of what we call the "Prospects of Mankind." We are doing this study from four points of view. First, simply as a kind of academic exercise and general continuation of our interest in medium and long-term futures; secondly, to get some sense of the degree, the current pessimism (or what is sometimes called a "failure of nerve") is actually justified. Third, to see to what degree one can use these long-term images of the future as a kind of ideology or perspective in which one can make more likely higher levels of peace, prosperity, freedom, quality of life, and justice. Fourth and finally, to consciously adopt the perspective of our grandchildren and great-grandchildren. There is little or nothing in the current system that systematically discounts much more than ten or twenty years. It is quite conceivable that we today are doing things that will hurt greatly the prospects of our descendants. I myself do not believe that this fourth study is going to develop many extraordinarily new or interesting items, but it seems to me that even a mini-mum sense of responsibility requires us to a prolonged effort of such study in general—and in particular into study of what I call "far-fetched and probably nonexist-ent but very important problems if they occur." Some of these are discussed very briefly in my own paper in this volume when I talk about the 1985 technological crisis.

I can briefly summarize our current position by say-ing that we can find no crucially important physical barri-ers to the coming of the postindustrial society, indeed among the first results already achieved by the project I include a quite surprising one. When we started the study we assumed that we would have to argue that in order to meet these difficult problems of the future, we would have to depend upon new technologies being created and adopted, and that while we might be able to argue quite persuasively that we could indeed be sure that these new technologies would be forthcoming, it would be basically an act of faith. However, as near as we can see, modern technology has now developed to the point, particularly in the last twenty years, that we can now say that even if limited to existing (and in hand) technology there should be no cataclysmic simple re-source restraints. That is, if one doesn't worry about undesired byproducts (such as sulfur dioxide when coal is burned or a kind of social malaise that may come with more affluence), then as far as we can tell there are no likely simple overwhelming resource constraints.

Formulating this last thought a little more carefully, we can say that as far as currently perceived and felt pollution and similar issues are concerned we seem likely to be able to deal with them in the long run at reasonable costs—at least in the scenarios we feel likely—or even in some of the more difficult possibilities (for example, assume that the world population stabilizes at about twenty billion people and at an income level of about fifteen thousand dollars per capita or at a total World Gross Product of more than 300 trillion dollars some time in the twenty-first century). Nor do there seem to be impossible decision problems requiring world government or similar organization. Nor, as far as we can tell, are there necessarily going to be catastrophic political issues associated with, for example, increasing gaps between the rich and the poor and so on for the list of looming disasters that current discussion emphasizes so much. None of the above is to say that serious tragedies could not occur—including even some ultimate worldwide cataclysm. It is only to say that the current arguments for near inevitability of such problems as so many neo-Malthusians would argue are most unpersuasive—and the contrary arguments can be made relatively persuasive. Indeed, in most cases, relatively plausible projections can be made that indicate that most of these problems will not arise at all in the form that is usually described.

In this volume we are focusing attention on business in the next decade or so. These neo-Malthusian issues will not come to a head in that period. Of course, if it were really true that in fifty to one hundred years we really will be running into catastrophes of limited resources or of pollution or environmental problems, then we should not act in the way implied by the discussion. Thus the United States is often described as having only six per cent of the world's population and using up one-third of the world's "irreplaceable" resources. This is then described as being like taking a public shower in the last barrel of water on a life raft when everybody else is dying of thirst.

Even though we argue that these theoretical catastrophes in fifty to a hundred years will likely not arise or be dealt with, there will be some very catastrophic issues or situations arising, and some of them in the same period under discussion—i.e., in the next decade or two. We call the set of issues associated with these possibilities the "1985 technological crisis," as discussed very briefly in my paper and later in general. In other words, we are not taking here a Pollyannic or optimistic position —in some ways the opposite in saying that if the problems do arise then they may arise not in fifty or a hundred years from now but may arise very soon. However, we also feel if we get through this "1985 technological crisis" then there is good reason for believing we can do reasonably well in the future. Of course, all problems are never settled permanently; there will be problems in the long-term future also.

But let me turn now to the most basic assumptions that obviously almost all the contributors had and which I think were perfectly correct: that our problems are most likely to be those that will be associated with afflu-

ence rather than those of poverty, misery, deadly pollution, and resource shortages. This basic concept is very
well expressed in the first paper by Bell, and this is why
it is in some ways the most important paper in the sym-
posium. Despite differences of approach and emphasis,
there was general agreement on many other broad issues
as well. A consensus emerged—at least in my view—that
to survive and prosper in the seventies, the business
corporation will have to cope successfully with a pro-
foundly changing economic, social, and political environment.

Among the trends and issues that currently seem of
special interest in these speculations and that may affect
the future of the corporation significantly is the fact that
per capita incomes in the United States and parts of
Europe are approaching post-industrial levels (i.e., more
than $5,000). Along with this is a corresponding change
in values, attitudes, and life styles of individuals and a
great increase in domestic and international economic
activity—particularly, on the one hand, trade, foreign
investment, and multinational corporations, and, on the
other, an enormous growth in what I have called "quaternary activities"—i.e., tourism, sports, play, retirement,
education for "fun" or other personal purposes, various
literary, aesthetic, artistic, religious, and public-service
activities, other paths to "self-actualization," services to
such quaternary activities, and, of course, services to
such quaternary services.

This is, of course, accompanied by a declining role
of the production-oriented economy—i.e., extractive,
such as agriculture, forestry, fishing and hunting activities (primary); manufacturing and construction (second-

ary); services to primary and secondary activities (tertiary); and services to tertiary services (also tertiary)—with first the emergence and eventually the domination of the "quaternary" economy which, as suggested above, is based on final demands by consumers for products that are relatively removed from the "necessities of life" and from primary, secondary, or tertiary activities and purposes; services to such "nonessential consumption" activities and purposes; and services to such services.

There are also certain striking cultural changes or tendencies that on the surface sometimes seem matters of changing fashions or transient political controversies, but that may go deeper. Thus, the emerging ecological, "zero-growth," and/or "consumerism" consciousness, as well as the more dramatic political and youth protest and dropout groups may all be symptomatic of relatively deep and permanent changes, first in elite and eventually in popular values and attitudes. These affect particularly values and attitudes associated with economic rationalism and scientific and technological progress and, by analogy, with certain assumptions of human and social progress that have been dynamic factors in the evolution of modern society. All these seem likely in turn to lead to:

1. Emphasis on the technology and other requirements of social and environmental engineering and on stricter and more explicit criteria relating to health, safety, recreation, self-actualization, aesthetics, etc., as they affect both the employees of the corporation and the community at large.

2. Growing importance of neoeconomic incentives

(employee interest in neighborhood, schooling, product, fringe benefits, interpersonal relations, organizational "personality" and ambience, and degree of participatory "democracy" and/or of decentralization—a less overwhelming if still great interest in salary and possibilities for advancement).

3. Greater dependence on consensual techniques, information transfer, and even "participatory democracy" rather than classical use of rules, orders, directives, and "top down" command and control. Tension between simultaneous tendencies toward decentralization and centralization. Periodic corporate reorganizations as a way of life. At the extreme, greater emphasis on "consentive" (participatory and voluntary) and even "anarchic" (self-actualization-oriented) rather than hierarchical (command and authority-oriented) bureaucracies.

4. Some reaction against mass-consumption values and orientations—some erosion of work-oriented, advancement-oriented, achievement-oriented business values—and some overreaction—perhaps in both directions.

5. Loss of traditional "levers" (i.e., religion, tradition, economic and military pressures, etc.) and a consequent search for "meaning and purpose."

6. Development of pluralistic and mosaic subcultures exhibiting a diversity of life styles—many esoteric, exotic, communal, and utopian enclaves and subcultures—however, probably with appreciable mobility between the enclaves and subcultures, and from

them to "square life" (including corporate life). Clothes and styles of life are likely to reflect basic philosophy, role, vocation, and/or avocational choices, with little imitation (or even a rejection) of traditional upper- and middle-class styles.

7. Rise of a "learning society" (including, in business, much use of "computer-assisted instruction for management skills as well as job skills: with perhaps 5–10 per cent of the organization "taking special formal courses" and almost everybody participating in "information and orientation" activities). Relative emphasis on late knowledge, courage, innovation, and imagination. Increased number and importance in corporate life of "job skipping" problem-oriented executives.

8. Other manifestations of a coming "post-industrial" society which is not yet post-economic or post-business.

Another important development has to do with rapidly changing technologies and operating practices. There are likely to be new products, new markets, new organizations, new forms of competition, continued emphasis on large organizations and complex institutions despite the current "revolt against bureaucracy." However, small countries and small but flexible and innovative organizations may do exceedingly well—in particular, if they can also generate communal motivation and a sense of overall responsibility.

Automatic data processing will probably be used to generate "real time" national income, wealth, social and environmental accounts and, to some degree, real time centralized national control and coordination. Some of the ingredients that could go into these purposes and activities include:

1. National Data Center on individuals and private and public organizations, with accompanying efficiencies of public administration and dilemmas of social control and technocratic or even police authoritarianism.

2. Many other special data centers—e.g., for specific industries, for multinational purposes, and for other private and public purposes.

3. Computerized country-wide and even worldwide buying, selling, and other transfers. Instantaneous or periodic but automatic and computerized payments, credit authorizations and advances, other money transfers and accounting. Corresponding political, legal, and social changes.

4. Many new, controlled and uncontrolled, international, national and local feedback mechanisms. Increasing worldwide effective economic unity.

5. Pervasive use of instantaneous or periodic but automatic calculation, analysis and display of status of various other processes, systems, and institutions.

6. Automatic and objective credit appraisal. Potential creditors have new legal rights and potential lenders have equivalent new obligations and perhaps vice versa.

7. Many national economies or sectors becoming almost checkless and, except for small sums, cashless.

8. At the limit, automated country-wide and even worldwide arbitrage—and thus many "perfect" (or near-perfect) markets in both goods and money and perhaps labor.

9. Use of computers to translate simple specialized documents—i.e., business forms, maintenance manuals, commercial documents, etc.

Distant markets and suppliers seem likely to be increasingly important—both in foreign trade and in foreign plants and the development of special equipment, services, organizations, and institutions to further these activities, e.g.:

1. Mobile and portable "field offices" which use small (even briefcase-sized) computers, commercially available data links, and highly sophisticated information-retrieval systems with perhaps enough remotely controlled office and design equipment, and video communications to give this field office many of the technical and administrative capabilities of the home office.

2. New roles for newly developing "industrial" and "mass-consumption" societies in relationship to both the more-advanced and the less-advanced societies—including the development of new kinds of multinational "division of labor"—e.g., various service industries, personal services, maintenance and repair activities, and perhaps most important of all

for some areas, instead of bringing foreign workers to labor-short areas, there will be a tendency to send the work to where the labor is—likelihood that the multinational concern will play a central role in all the above.

3. New varieties of international, binational, and multinational profit-making and not-for-profit corporations and consortiums.

4. Also—and rather paradoxically—new possibilities for relative national—or even local—autarchy.

5. Enormous increase in tourism and distant, even multinational, "commuting" or geographical splitting of one's major areas of activities and responsibilities.

Many changes in the work/income relationship are in prospect, such as many part-time and/or intermittent workers; sabbaticals common; and some form of guaranteed annual income (explicit, covert, ambiguous, or intermediate) in the developing countries.

Finally, there will be many new issues, or old issues intensified in significance, such as:

1. Occasional mistakes, accidents, and even disasters due to excessive dependence on complex and highly centralized information systems or to malfunctions or accidents to large plants or vehicles (e.g., the 1,000-MW reactor, the million-pound plane, the million-ton tanker, and so on).

2. Also some deliberate (covert or open) misuse of information systems—by both public officials and

private individuals—and pressures toward development of a system of "due process" to protect individuals from such misuse.

3. On the one hand, a tendency toward inertia and a failure to generate anticipatory understandings and reactions to the many changes and to new or intensified problems, and on the other a value confusion which results in equally strong tendencies toward overacceptance of the new, toward "illusioned thinking," and toward greater prevalence of "trained incapacities," with particular emphasis on the growth of such "illusion" and "incapacity" in upper and upper-middle classes, intellectuals, management, and their young.

4. Many new issues of personal choice and public policy posed by new technologies such as organ transplants, genetic intervention, psychopharmacology, electronic surveillance, large-scale data processing, environmental degradation, and so on. Many of these will affect business and businessmen, some in surprising ways.

Will our post-industrial society also be a post-business society? That is an open issue. In the United States today there seems to be a tendency for corporate business to consider seriously entering many areas that have been traditionally the responsibility of government or the private individual. These areas include education, urban renewal, pollution, environment control, city planning, care of the old, hospitals, health and medical care generally, and so on. There does not seem to be very much of a tendency of this sort in Europe. Thus one can argue that if business largely stays in the same areas in which it is today, the post-industrial culture will also be post-business. If business moves heavily into new areas, and this seems likely in the United States, but perhaps less likely in Europe, then the post-industrial culture may not be post-business. Thus, there may be a big difference developing here between Europe and the United States. Of course, in practice, it is more likely to be a question of degree, a question of more so and less so. One should also point out that in a completely different area, the multinational corporation, business in both Europe and America is showing a new creativity, a new vitality, a new dynamism, and a new area of promise. As Dan Bell and Peter Drucker made clear, this is a very vital area indeed, and may be the clue to the even more rapid dissemination of technology, industry, and higher rates of development to the undeveloped and less-developed parts of the world than even the most optimistic recent estimates would suggest.